THE WAY OF THE TIGER

Edited by Colin Baxter Photography
Designed by Colin Baxter Photography
Printed in Hong Kong

First hardcover edition
01   02   03   04   05   5   4   3   2   1

First softcover edition
05   06   07   5   4

Library of Congress Cataloging-in-Publication Data

Karanth, Ullas.
The way of the tiger : natural history and conservation of the endangered big cat / Ullas Karanth.
p. cm. -- (A WorldLife discovery guide)
ISBN 0-89658-560-3
ISBN 0-89658-010-5 (pbk.)
1. Tigers. 2. Wildlife conservation. 1. Title. II. Series.
QL737.C23 K38 2001
599.756--dc21
2001026104

Distributed in Canada by Raincoast Books, 9050 Shaughnessy Street, Vancouver, B.C. V6P 6E5

Published by Voyageur Press, Inc.
123 North Second Street, P.O. Box 338, Stillwater, MN 55082 U.S.A.
651-430-2210, fax 651-430-2211
books@voyageurpress.com   www.voyageurpress.com

Educators, fundraisers, premium and gift buyers, publicists, and marketing managers:
Looking for creative products and new sales ideas? Voyageur Press books are available at special discounts when purchased in quantities, and special editions can be created to your specifications. For details contact the marketing department at 800-888-9653.

Photography © 2001 by:

Front cover © John Shaw (Bruce Coleman Inc)
Back cover (top left) © Belinda Wright (Oxford Scientific Films)
Back cover (top right) © Andy Rouse (NHPA)
Back cover (bottom) © Rod Williams (Bruce Coleman Collection)
Page 1 © Schafer & Hill (Still Pictures)
Page 4 © Gavriel Jecan (Art Wolfe Inc)
Page 6 © Art Wolfe (Art Wolfe Inc)
Page 7 © Ullas Karanth
Page 9 © John Shaw (Bruce Coleman Collection)
Page 10 © Lynn Stone (BBC Natural History Unit)
Page 12 © Francois Gohier (Ardea London Ltd)
Page 13 © Art Wolfe (Art Wolfe Inc)
Page 14 © Alain Compost (Bruce Coleman Collection)
Page 17 © M Watson (Ardea London Ltd)
Page 18 © Art Wolfe (Art Wolfe Inc)
Page 20 © Ullas Karanth
Page 21 © Bruce Coleman Inc (Bruce Coleman Collection)
Page 22 © Art Wolfe (Art Wolfe Inc)
Page 25 © Eric Dragesco (Ardea London Ltd)
Page 26 top © Klein/Hubert (Still Pictures)
Page 26 bottom © Klein/Hubert (Still Pictures)
Page 28 © Gerald Lacz (Still Pictures)
Page 29 © Heather Angel
Page 30 © Anup Shah (BBC Natural History Unit)
Page 33 left © Masahiro Iijima (Ardea London Ltd)
Page 33 right © Masahiro Iijima (Ardea London Ltd)
Page 35 © Joe McDonald (Bruce Coleman Inc)
Page 36 © Len Rue Jr

Page 38 © Tony Stone Worldwide
Page 39 © Tom Brakefield (Bruce Coleman Inc)
Page 41 © Tom & Pat Leeson
Page 42 © Tim Fitzharris (Minden Pictures)
Page 45 © Leonard Lee Rue III
Page 46 © John Shaw (Bruce Coleman Inc)
Page 49 © Manoj Shah (Tony Stone Images)
Page 50 © Anup Shah (BBC Natural History Unit)
Page 51 © Anup Shah (BBC Natural History Unit)
Page 53 © Jeffrey Rich (Nature Photography)
Page 54 © Joe McDonald (Bruce Coleman Inc)
Page 57 © Anup Shah (BBC Natural History Unit)
Page 58 © Andy Rouse (NHPA)
Page 61 © Joanna Van Gruiven (Ardea)
Page 62 © Art Wolfe (Art Wolfe Inc)
Page 65 © Ardea London Ltd
Page 66 © Len Rue Jr
Page 69 © M Watson (Ardea London Ltd))
Page 70 © E A Kuttapan (BBC Natural History Unit)
Page 73 © E A Kuttapan (BBC Natural History Unit)
Page 74 © Bruce Coleman Inc
Page 77 © Rodney Griffiths
Page 78 © Mike Hill (Oxford Scientific Films)
Page 80 © Andy Rouse (NHPA)
Page 81 © Chris Brunskill (Ardea London Ltd)
Page 82 © M Watson (Ardea London Ltd)
Page 85 © Rod Williams (Bruce Coleman Collection)
Page 86 © Art Wolfe (Art Wolfe Inc)

Page 88 © Masahiro Iijima (Ardea London Ltd)
Page 89 © Staffan Widstrand (BBCD Natural History Unit)
Page 90 © James Warwick (NHPA)
Page 92 © David Higgs (The Environmental Press Agency)
Page 93 left © Steve Galstor (The Environmental Press Agency)
Page 93 right © David Higgs (TEPA)
Page 94 © Manoj Shah (Tony Stone Images)
Page 97 © J P Zwaenepoel (Bruce Coleman Collection)
Page 99 © Rodney Griffiths
Page 100 © Chris Brunskill (Ardea London Ltd)
Page 103 © Art Wolfe (Art Wolfe Inc)
Page 104 © D&T Images
Page 105 © David Higgs (TEPA)
Page 106 © Art Wolfe (Art Wolfe Inc)
Page 108 © Tom & Pat Leeson
Page 111 © Rodney Griffiths
Page 113 © Jorg & Petra Wegner
Page 114 © Ann & Steve Toon
Page 117 © Masahiro Iijima (Ardea London Ltd)
Page 118 © Art Wolfe (Tony Stone Images)
Page 121 © Tom & Pat Leeson
Page 122 © M Watson (Ardea London Ltd)
Page 124 © Joanna Van Gruiven (Ardea London Ltd)
Page 125 © Tom & Pat Leeson
Page 126 © Alan & Sandy Carey (Tony Stone Images)
Page 129 © Andy Rouse (NHPA)

THE WAY OF THE TIGER

Natural History and Conservation of the Endangered Big Cat

K. Ullas Karanth

Voyageur Press

Contents

For Prathibha and Krithi.

Introduction

An Encounter with Wild Tigers

It was a cold morning in May 1994. I drove my battered 4X4 along the grass-covered forest track cleaving through the curtain of mist that still enveloped the forests. Dew dripped heavily from the foliage. A jungle fowl puffed up his silver hackles and crowed: *Kick yaa. Kick-kick*, he announced his intentions boldly to rival cocks, from a safe perch on an *Erythrina* sapling. With me were two men from a British television crew, hoping to film tigers. We were in Nagarahole, a green jewel of a wildlife park at the foot of the Western Ghat Mountains in the Indian state of Karnataka. Teeming with deer, pigs and gaur on which tigers prey, this dense jungle is a paradise for the big cats. However, I thought our chances of actually seeing a tiger, let alone filming one, were pretty slim; unlike in the open forests of some north Indian parks, where tourists can view some habituated tigers, the cats of Nagarahole are secretive and shy.

I was proved wrong soon enough. As we came up a rise, I spotted a bulky form silhouetted against the mist, about 250 ft (75 meters) ahead. A tigress sat on the road, facing us. Her two cubs, slightly smaller than leopards, were playing in front of her. Tigers in the mist! It was a marvelous family portrait of the great cats, their rich ochre and black colors subtly showing through the white veil swirling around them. I stopped the vehicle and cut the engine.

The tigress lay down, still facing us. She was alert but calm. The cubs gambolled in the short grass. Blue-winged parakeets and black hill mynas screeched around us. An unwary peacock walked towards the tigress from behind, spotted her suddenly, and flew away, emitting raucous alarm calls. Nothing seemed to bother the tigers; we watched them for over 40 minutes and the TV crew, feeling ever-more confident, had their fill of exceptional footage of wild tigers.

The cubs, still playing, got closer and closer to us. Suddenly,

Tigers in the mist in Nagarahole.

something – maybe the whirr of the video camera – alarmed the tigress. She stood up and started cantering towards us: eyes blazing, ears erect, strides quickening. I realized that she was going to charge; but, having spent nearly a decade studying tigers, I also knew that we were perfectly safe inside the vehicle, and that she would veer off during the last second of her mock charge. She was merely warning us to get away from her cubs.

My hitherto confident companions, however, were in a panic. It was the first time they had seen a charging tigress – surely their last one too, they seemed to think, certain that the open vehicle provided no protection against her fury. Whispering,

The tiger is an obligate carnivore that hunts large ungulates through stealth.

I managed to calm them, and they restrained themselves from jumping off the vehicle.

Within seconds the tigress charged, emitting blood-curdling growls and bounding to within 10 ft (3 meters) of us, before swerving off to the left. She continued to growl menacingly from within the dense bamboo cover, as her cubs scurried back up the track. I reversed the vehicle a few yards to reassure her, and the growls subsided. While my companions had become nervous wrecks, I had enjoyed the spectacular show of feline ferocity; not because I was any braver than they were, but because my perception of the moment was shaped by what I knew about tiger behavior. The TV crew had merely reacted with the elemental fear most people instinctively feel for the great cat.

The fear of tigers is deeply rooted in our biological and social history, and it is easy to understand why we humans have tried, all too successfully, to eliminate the dreaded predator. It is a little harder to understand why we have tried to save an animal that we fear so much.

As a schoolboy interested in wild animals during the 1960s, I saw India's forests and wildlife vanishing rapidly. Convinced that their splendid wild animals would soon disappear, I decided to watch animals as often as I could in the jungles of my neighborhood in southwestern India. I did not think I would ever see my favorite animal, the tiger, in these forests.

In 1967, I rode my motorcycle to Nagarahole Game Sanctuary. 'Game' was scarce even in the legally protected 'sanctuary'. Gunshots echoed through the night as villagers prowled the forests looking for deer meat. Snares were laid across forest trails; squatters encroached into the forests to grow rice, while their cattle grazed down the vegetation and loggers felled great swathes of the jungles. Here I met a forester named Kotrangada Chinnappa, who had just begun to confront these pressures with uncommon grit and determination. I kept coming back, getting deeply involved in the conservation of Nagarahole over the years.

By the mid 1970s, things were looking up for wildlife in India, as a result of efforts of men like Chinnappa who were enforcing the new conservation laws. At this time, I read a book called *The Deer and the Tiger*, which described wildlife biologist George Schaller's pioneering tiger study in central India. Instantly, I felt like someone with defective vision putting on corrective glasses; the blurry portraits of tigers painted by old hunters came into sharp focus under Schaller's scientific lens. I knew this was exactly what I *had* to do in my own life. I eventually went to study wildlife biology at the University of Florida under the tutelage of Melvin Sunquist. In 1988, I returned to Nagarahole to renew my quest for reliable knowledge about tigers, a quest that continues to this day.

Like politics, tiger conservation is the art of the possible, but its full potential can be realized only if our actions are based on a solid foundation of knowledge. There is no sure-fire way of predicting how successful we will ultimately be, but the more sensibly we act now, the greater is the chance that the tiger will survive the twenty-first century. Mere doomsday prophesies, however well-intentioned, discourage rational conservation action, and may be harming rather than helping the tigers' cause. My view is that, on the basis of biological facts and historical background, the tiger is not yet a lost cause.

My goal is to convince conservationists that wild tigers can indeed survive the twenty-first century if we can temper our compassion for the animal with knowledge and pragmatism. I also hope to share some of the excitement and pleasure I have derived from studying wild tigers in India.

Tigers occasionally like to sun themselves.

Why Save Tigers?

Saving wild tigers in an overpopulated world now means locking up productive farmland in wildlife reserves, and suffering occasional depredations by the big cat on livestock and even human beings. Yet, for over a quarter of a century now, we have kept up the efforts to save wild tigers. Is this rational behavior on our part? Why should we try to save tigers when so many other urgent human problems demand our attention?

Ecologists who study the earth's ecosystems and try to model their dynamics argue that the plant and animal communities that share our planet contribute to the stability and functioning of biological and chemical cycles that make life possible for us on this planet. Ecological modeller Simon Levin compares the earth's biosphere to a 'self organizing, complex adaptive system' in which each little cluster of component parts influences the overall functioning of the system through feed back loops. He suggests that loss of species could have unpredictable and possibly dangerous consequences for us. Ecologist David Tillman argues that biological diversity itself may provide stability to our ecosystems.

Population biologist Paul Ehrlich illustrates the danger of potential species losses, with a dramatic example: the ecosystem is like an airplane in which we are passengers. We can go on removing the rivets that hold the plane's wings up, one by one, for quite a while. While no single rivet may determine when we will crash, ultimately one particular rivet surely will. Each species that becomes extinct is like one more rivet pulled out from our plane.

Going beyond such arguments that urge prudence for the sake of the future, we can see that tiger habitats provide us with tangible benefits even now. The forests that clothe the tiger's habitats are also watersheds of major Asian river systems such as the Ganga, Brahmaputra, Irrawaddy and Mekong. These forests regulate the flow of water after the seasonal rains and protect the soil underneath from erosion. The survival of these forests is therefore critical to the welfare of millions of farmers who depend on these rivers. When we protect tiger forests from logging, overgrazing, fires and conversion to cropland, we are not indulging in a luxury that we cannot afford in a poverty-stricken, overpopulated world. We are, in fact, protecting the soil-water resources that sustain millions of people in Asia.

These tiger forests are also treasure troves of biological diversity. They harbor millions of species of plants, insects, amphibians, reptiles, birds and mammals. These life forms took millions of years to evolve; we have only just begun to document their extraordinary variety and diversity. Consequently, we barely understand the complex ecological linkages among these plants and animals: certainly not enough to predict how the elimination of one species may affect the fate of others.

Often, extermination of species can disrupt links between predators and prey, flowers and pollinators, fruits and the dispersers of their seeds. Collecting specimens in museums, arboretums and zoos cannot prevent these cascading effects of species extinctions. Wild plants and animals have to be primarily saved wherever they occur in the living landscapes around us. Tigers are an integral part of these complex ecosystems.

The diversity of plant and animal life needs to be preserved because of the immense current benefits and future gains that it can bring to us. Most of our crop plants and domestic animals are bred from wild relatives and can potentially benefit greatly

Wide padded feet allow tigers to negotiate the snow in the Russian Far East.

from the vast, barely tapped wild gene pools. Many of our current drugs, as well as sources of energy, fibers and structural materials, come from a few exploited species that we have discovered. As biotechnology becomes an increasingly important weapon in our fight against hunger, homelessness, poverty and disease, the role of those as yet undiscovered life

Tigers are sometimes active in the daytime.

forms will become even more central to our own welfare. Yet the natural habitats that harbor potentially useful life forms are being lost every day in a massive extinction spasm that we have inflicted on nature. Sometimes, we humans seem determined to burn this unique insurance policy that nature has generously provisioned for our future.

Wild tigers are the warning lamps that indicate how healthy

natural landscapes continue to remain in the face of our onslaught; their survival is as useful to us as the oil-pressure lamp on the dashboard of a car or the battery life indicator on a laptop computer.

The remaining tiger habitats are wonderful laboratories of nature, an irreplaceable library of life. They possess, in a large measure, what conservationist William Conway calls 'nature's ability to surprise us'. In these we can study nature at work and benefit from the knowledge we gain. In its attempts to destroy remnants of such forests to meet some temporary need, human society seems to be behaving like a mob of illiterates bent on burning down an ancient library.

Moreover, the wild landscapes that now harbor tigers comprise less than five per cent of the land in most tiger range countries. One cannot imagine any pressing problem faced by the three-billion strong population in Asia, getting solved by sacrificing these nature reserves. Problems such as poverty, landlessness, hunger, disease and social discrimination have remained intractable over centuries. Their ultimate solution lies in using the remaining 95 per cent of the land outside the reserves wisely.

Apart from such practical reasons, there are also ethical and esthetic reasons for saving wild tigers. Tigers, and the plant and animal communities that sustain them, are products of millions of years of natural evolution. Don't they have a right to survive and evolve as nature intended them to, at least in some parts of the once-green earth that we have so drastically modified?

The tiger is undoubtedly one of the most beautiful of all nature's creations, and has inspired human cultures over millennia. No one has expressed the ethical and esthetic imperative for saving wild tigers more eloquently than biologist George Schaller, who said in 1993: 'Future generations would be truly saddened that this century had so little foresight, so little compassion, such lack of generosity of spirit for the future

Tigers on the Indonesian island Sumatra belong to a distinct subspecies. They live
in tropical evergreen rainforests. They are much smaller than the tigers on mainland Asia and
possess richly colored coats with the stripes spaced closer together.

that it would eliminate one of the most beautiful and dramatic animals that the world has ever seen'.

Critical Questions in Tiger Conservation

For all the above reasons, the world's scientific community, most governments, conservation agencies and a wide section of the public agree that saving rare, extinction-prone species, such as the tiger, is a global necessity from both practical and moral considerations. The consensus on this issue is remarkably broad, and cuts across political, ideological, national, and cultural boundaries. Even more remarkably, this consensus has crystallized within a relatively short period during the last quarter century. However, all this does not make the actual task of tiger conservation any less difficult. While there is agreement as to why we should save tigers, there are widely diverging views on how we should go about doing so. Many vexed questions are raised and debated.

Should we advocate policies that promote the coexistence of tiger populations amidst human settlements, or should we strive for separating the two as much as we can? To what extent are activities such as agriculture, raising livestock and collecting forest products compatible with tiger conservation goals? Can economic development projects be reconciled with tiger conservation? Is the international trade in tiger body parts the most important factor driving the tigers' decline, or is it the depletion of the tigers' prey base by local villagers? Should tiger habitats be managed by decentralized local authorities or by organized governmental efforts? Should we emphasize tough law enforcement to protect tigers or should we focus on people-friendly policies that keep the tiger's human neighbors happy? Should we motivate local people to save tigers through commercial incentives or by appealing to their sense of local pride, culture or tradition? Do we need more or less money to go into tiger conservation schemes? How important are the issues of genetics and captive breeding for saving wild tigers? How can captive tigers help wild ones? How do we measure success or failure in tiger conservation: by the amount of money we spend, the welfare provided to local people or by actually going out and counting wild tigers? Are we succeeding or failing in our collective efforts to save tigers? Is the tiger a lost cause, or is there some reason for hope?

The Role of Reliable Knowledge

The answers to these questions differ widely, but in the end, they boil down to two things: which conservation activities should be emphasized and what proportion of resources should be allocated to each. Different conservation prescriptions arise from differences in perceptions about what wild tigers need and about our own impacts on these needs. Much of the discord arises because of a lack of reliable knowledge about tigers. To illustrate this, let us look at some opinions that are widely shared among the world's tiger conservationists.

It is often stated that there were 40,000 tigers in India at the beginning of the twentieth century and that only 3000 or 5000, or some other number, survive now. The first number is merely an opinion expressed by a naturalist 40 years ago, and the latter numbers are only guesses without any solid basis. Yet these so-called 'facts' have gained wide currency through repetition in the world's media.

Another famous, oft-repeated quote is that the largest contiguous wild tiger population in the world today survives in the Sundarban delta in India and Bangladesh. In fact, mangrove forest is a poor-quality tiger habitat, with apparently low prey densities. Recent studies suggest that the high tiger numbers reported are more likely to be the result of poor counting methods. Although a unique and important habitat, Sundarbans are unlikely to support the largest contiguous tiger population in the world.

It is widely believed that originally there were eight subspecies of tigers, and only five of these survive now. However, recent studies suggest that there were only three 'subspecies', and two of these survive now. All the tigers on mainland Asia appear to belong to just one subspecies, while tigers in Sumatra belong to the other.

Many people think that white tigers are a rare variety that needs to be conserved. Actually, white tigers are genetic mutants derived by repeatedly crossbreeding the progeny derived from a single wild-caught ancestor. While white tigers are undoubtedly rather cute oddities, they have little conservation value.

It is often believed that tigers in captivity provide stock for reintroductions into the wild. The fact is that it is more cost-effective to protect habitats so that wild tiger populations can recover, compared to raising expensive captive tigers that have little hope of finding suitable new habitats for reintroductions.

Let us take the bland assertion that in Asia, tigers have happily coexisted with local people over thousands of years. It then follows that policies that make local people unhappy by restricting farming, livestock raising and the collection of forest products in critical tiger habitats are unnecessary to maintain viable breeding tiger populations in the future. The reality, however, is that during this period of allegedly happy coexistence in the past, the distributional range of breeding tiger populations has probably shrunk to one per cent of its former size. For the tigers at least, the history of coexistence has not been a happy experience.

Look at the dire prediction, made in 1993 by many of the world's leading tiger conservationists, and repeated by the media (including *Time* magazine and the BBC) that wild tigers were in deep trouble and would go extinct by the year 2000. While wild tigers continued to be in trouble in the year 2000, they were certainly not extinct. There is a chance that tigers may indeed survive the twenty-first century, at least in some parts of their range.

It can be seen from these examples that many of the differences in possible approaches to saving tigers arise because of lack of reliable knowledge. Two basic biological traits of tigers — large size and carnivorous diet — impinge on every conservation decision we have to make now. Therefore, a major part of this book is necessarily about tiger biology.

Understanding the tiger's biological needs so that we can accommodate them — to the extent we can — in our vastly complicated agenda for human progress is a crucial part of the conservation enterprise. Gaining such understanding through the application of science is therefore essential for the process of conservation. Science derives its strength because, as a philosopher said, 'science works'. Science works in the real world because of the methods it employs to gain knowledge. Therefore, in this book I have also tried to explain the methods that scientists use to study tigers. Rigorous methods and evaluation of the results are what set tiger science clearly apart from tiger lore, legend and hunters' tales.

However, tiger conservation is an activity that we humans undertake — not the tigers themselves. Therefore, tiger conservation must involve a human dimension. The social, economic and cultural dimensions of conservation cannot be ignored by anyone seriously working to save tigers. Tigers have inspired humanity from its pre-historic past through historical times to the modern days. They were worshipped as deities by primitive cultures and have been royal mascots. Tigers are now in corporate logos that sell a variety of products from ice cream to sports cars. Our primary challenge is to channel this human fascination for the tiger into positive conservation action.

Tigers like to cool off by lying in water.

Enduring Fascination

Tigers in Ancient History

Thousands of years ago, primitive humans scurried around in the underbrush of the Asian forests, digging for roots, picking up berries and snaring smaller animals. A giant predator, five times their size, stalked them. Armed with fearsome teeth and claws, moving silently like a shadow through the darkness of the night, the beast inspired both fear and admiration in our primitive ancestors. Its great muscular form, lithe grace, spectacular coloration and symmetry of form, all added to its mystique. Thus, the fascination for tigers is deeply rooted within us. No wonder that the tiger has been worshipped as a deity in traditional tribal and animistic cultures of Asia, ranging from the snowy Russian Far East to the steamy jungles in Java.

This awe of the tiger persisted in the human psyche even after early agriculturists managed to tame the tiger's jungles through fire, and inventions such as the axe and the plow. Since historic times, the tiger has been revered as a deity in legends and myths of Asia. The animal's name was synonymous with valor and power, and its presence ubiquitous in Hindu, Buddhist and Islamic iconography. Tigers proliferated in art and folklore. As a result, tragically for the tiger, the animal's body parts came to be perceived as cure-all remedies among the medicine men of the orient.

A 5000-year-old seal from the Indus valley civilization in South Asia depicts a man sitting on a tree addressing a tiger waiting for him below. With the spread of Hinduism, and later its offshoot Buddhism, from India into southeast Asia and China, the tiger continued to proliferate in the iconography of the orient.

India's early Dravidian deities like Male-Mahadeswara in Karnataka and Ayyappan in Kerala are depicted riding the striped predator; the tiger is worshipped as Dakshin Ray by honey hunters of Bengal, as Bagh Deo by tribes in Madhya Pradesh and as Pili Bhootha by the peasantry along the Karnataka coast. In the Chinese calendar, every twelfth year is marked down as the 'Year of the Tiger'. In Korea, the tiger is deified as the mountain spirit and king of beasts. In Java and Bali ancient kings are believed to assume the form of tigers and live in sacred caves, to which people trek long distances and pay homage even to this day.

Huli Vesha: The Tiger Dance of India

The tiger dancers of southwestern India exemplify how the tiger still thrives in numerous folk arts all over Asia. Huli Vesha — literally meaning 'tiger masquerade' — is a folk ritual in the coastal districts of Karnataka State in India. During the festival of Dasara celebrated by Hindus to mark the slaying of an evil demon by goddess Durga, her devotees form troupes of 'tiger dancers'. Usually the lead tiger dancer performs the ritual to fulfil a vow made to the goddess, in return for a favor granted, such as recovery from an illness, or the birth of a child.

Wandering troupes of half a dozen men perform the tiger dance every day along the streets and by-lanes of towns and villages. Each performance lasts 15 to 20 minutes, and is accompanied by a band of percussion instruments that can be heard from miles away. The tiger dancers are trailed by hundreds of admiring fans, mostly local children and teenagers. The householder or the shopkeeper before whom the dancers perform, is obliged to pay them some money. The troupe then moves on. This routine goes on for nine festive days.

On the ninth evening, a gaudily painted, larger-than-life idol of

Tigers spend most of the day resting.

19

Durga is taken in a huge ceremonial procession to be immersed in the temple pond. All the tiger dance troupes in town, and other devotees masquerading as different characters, converge on this procession. At the end of the rituals, the tiger men wash off their body paint by bathing in the temple pond, and become normal human beings again.

These tiger dancers are usually heroes in their neighborhoods. Rivalry between troupes is often a serious matter. Consequently, tiger dance performances are often mixed with mutual challenges and counter-challenges involving feats of strength. Such feats may include the lead dancer biting a live goat with his front teeth and flipping it over his shoulders with a jerk of his head, like a real tiger does. Or it may involve him jumping across a wide and deep well, carrying the goat under his arm; the heavier the goat, the greater is the feat.

The traditional body painting of tiger dancers is an elaborate affair. The men are virtually naked, except for briefs. They lie down on large banana leaves and have their bodies painted by master artists. The painting takes hours to complete. If executed traditionally, the body painting superbly evokes the tiger's magnificent coloration and markings, accentuating its most striking features. Usually, the lead dancer wears a life-size, realistic tiger mask that covers his head. Around his waist he wears a long springy tail wrapped in real tiger skin.

The steps of the dancers emulate the tiger's natural gait remarkably faithfully. The careful stalk, the slouch-shouldered

Tiger dancer from India.

walk, grooming and paw-licking, two tigers facing off ferociously and the act of a tigress nursing her cubs, are all depicted with much vigor and realism, to the accompaniment of a drumbeat that keeps the spectators' pulses racing.

Unfortunately, with the increasing impact of television and films, which have corrupted most folk art traditions in India, the tiger dance too has suffered. The traditional styles of body painting, the mask, and the dance steps that I witnessed as a boy, have all succumbed to a hideous modernization process.

Changing Views of Tigers

The earliest record of tigers in Europe is of an animal brought to Athens by the Greek general Seloucus Nictor I, of the army of Alexander the Great. Thereafter, gladiators fought with captive tigers in Roman arenas. In the twelfth century King Henry I exhibited what may have been the first tiger in England, at his exclusive private menagerie at Oxford. Global traveller Marco Polo, who visited central Asia in 1300, recounted the prowess of the Mongol warriors who hunted 'striped lions' from horseback. The image of the big cat is invariably associated with the traits of power and valor, inspiring many an overweight potentate to title himself after the graceful cat.

The cultural fascination with the tiger continued, even after humans mastered technology, trade and commerce and dominated the tiger's domain through hunting, agriculture and industry. This fascination spread all over the world after the fifteenth century, when tigers were widely displayed in the

menageries of Europe. Spanish colonizers, who encountered another big cat that we now know as the jaguar in the New World, promptly called it *El Tigre*.

After firearms were invented, European rulers, native kings, landlords, planters, foresters, officials and other assorted adventurers swarmed the Asian forests, eager to slaughter tigers to prove that they were brave, rich or virile. Because members of these élite classes usually disliked the physical drudgery and danger involved in going after the elusive beast, vast numbers of recruits from the poorer social classes – tribesmen, trackers, and mahouts (elephant drivers) – were conscripted into the tiger-hunting enterprise. These humble men were mere cannon fodder: they erected shooting platforms, rode elephants, worked as beaters and even tracked dangerous, wounded tigers when their masters' shots went awry. For a while, in the 1950s and 1960s, inspired by African examples, even commercial safari hunting of tigers came into vogue.

The observations and beliefs of the native forest people, woven together with the literary skills of their upper-class masters, produced vast quantities of tiger lore during the last three centuries. As biologist George Schaller commented later, 'Although the literature on the tiger is voluminous, most of it is devoted to a discussion of how to shoot the animal, to arguments concerning its size and power to scent, and to interminable anecdotes about dangerous encounters with it'. Such views of the tiger, obtained along the barrel of a gun, provide us with a second set of portraits of the predator.

In these colonial-era portraits, the tiger lost its earlier supernatural, semi-divine aura, and acquired traits considered desirable in an upper-class man of the day. In this genre of writing, the tiger is commonly portrayed as a 'gentleman' – conjuring up for us visions of the big cat clad in khaki shorts, sipping Scotch on the veranda of a bungalow! In other contemporaneous accounts, like the one by nineteenth-century British hunter Charles Inglis, the tiger becomes 'an embodiment of devilish cruelty, of hate and savagery incarnate'. Similar thoughts echo in Rudyard Kipling's tale about the evil tiger Sher Khan. These portrayals, too, bear little resemblance to the true character of the big cat in the woods.

Tigers in Modern Culture

The human fascination for the tiger thrives to this day. The tiger is used as a potent brand image to sell anything from beer to gasoline, breakfast cereals to varnish paint. The tiger is the ruling icon of modern sports, too: it was the mascot of the Seoul Olympics and continues to be one for the sports teams at Princeton, Louisiana and Mississippi State Universities in the United States.

The tiger is the symbol of ideologically opposed political parties such as the Muslim League of Pakistan and the Hindu Shiv Sena in India. Many military units across the world have tigers as their mascots. The language of modern economics has succumbed to the tiger magic: several fast-growing nations in the Pacific Rim are called the 'Asian Tiger Economies'. Even mutual funds run by staid investment bankers are named after the exotic cat.

Tigers are among the most popular animals in zoos, circuses and menageries of all sorts. They even star in gaudy entertainment shows, such as those promoted by Las Vegas entertainers Siegfried and Roy. As a result of such public exposure, more people on earth have now seen tigers in the flesh, than at any other time in human history.

Tigers are a big-ticket attraction for the wildlife tourism industry in India and Nepal. Hundreds of thousands of visitors, both native and foreign, throng to reserves like Kanha, Ranthambore and Chitwan in the hope of catching a glimpse of wild, free-living tigers. Even as the fate of wild tigers hangs in the balance because of negative human impacts, fascination for the animal is burgeoning among human cultures across the world.

Understanding Tigers

After the eighteenth century, hunters, zoological collectors and naturalists strove to obtain more objective views of the tiger. As a result, a third set of tiger portraits, based partly on modern science, began to emerge. Detailed anatomical studies of tigers were made by zoologists to clarify evolutionary relationships among tigers, other cats, and other mammals. Reginald Pocock of the British Museum advanced this work significantly in the early twentieth century.

At the same time, a few hunter-naturalists began recording their observations on living tigers. Informative, if not wholly accurate, regional accounts of tigers were published by Nikolai Baikov in Russia, William Bazé in Indochina, and Arthur Locke in Malaya. Forester Dunbar Brander wrote about tiger behavior in central India while his colleague Fred Champion employed primitive camera traps to photograph tigers in the north. Jim Corbett, a part-time railway official and hunter-naturalist, made many perceptive observations on tigers, as he hunted down several man-eaters that had terrorized the rural populace in the Himalayan foothills of India.

Biological sciences of the twentieth century germinated from the seeds sown earlier by Swedish taxonomist Carl Linnaeus, British evolutionary biologist Charles Darwin and other pioneers. Ecology, the study of animals in relation to their environment, developed rapidly after the early 1900s, as did the study of animal behavior.

American forester Aldo Leopold pioneered modern wildlife management in the 1940s by applying the work of animal ecologists to address management issues. Wildlife management included preservation of species in decline, sustainable harvest of abundant species and even the regulation of wildlife pests.

In the decades after 1950, the practice of wildlife biology thrived in North America, Europe and the savannah regions of Africa. In the post-1980s period, the applied science of 'conservation biology', broader in scope than the old wildlife biology, appeared. Its vision extended beyond the earlier focus on terrestrial vertebrates, to cover general problems of conserving biological diversity at multiple scales: gene pools, populations, communities and landscapes.

In parallel with these developments in the second half of the twentieth century, modern-day biologists brought to bear new ideas, methods and tools to explore the world of the tiger. These scientific accounts of the magnificent predator are, I believe, even more fascinating than the tiger legends of earlier eras.

The Tiger Through the Eyes of Science

Although modern wildlife biology developed rapidly in the twentieth century, it did not make much headway among the hunters, naturalists and foresters in Asia, who played a dominant role in determining the tiger's fate. Consequently, even as late as the early 1960s, the ecology and behavior of wild tigers were scientifically undocumented.

In 1964, George Schaller, a biologist from the New York Zoological Society (now called the Wildlife Conservation Society), arrived at the remote Kanha reserve in central India to study tigers. The tools Schaller used to study tigers were rather rudimentary, and readily accessible to his Indian contemporaries: field notebooks, binoculars, cameras, and eight buffalo calves he bought from local villagers. However, Schaller brought to his task something additional that they lacked: a scientific framework of ecological inquiry.

Although Schaller spent barely 18 months in Kanha, his methodical, rigorous probing into the tiger's secret life hit a rich lode of information. This study is a testimony to Schaller's field skills, stamina and intellect. Published in 1967 under the

A tiger moves through its home range, searching for prey animals like deer and pigs. It initially locates its prey by sight or hearing, and then stalks it carefully. The tiger uses every bit of available cover to get close to the prey. It may remain frozen motionless, for long periods, when the quarry appears to be alert. The prey is usually knocked off its feet by the impact of the ferocious final charge, and the tiger simultaneously tries to bite the quarry's throat or neck.

Although hunting is an instinctive activity, a lot of learning is required before a tiger becomes a skillful hunter. Tiger cubs learn to hunt by observing their mother. They also indulge in a lot of rough play and mock aggression, acquiring in the process the skills to bring down large prey animals and to defend themselves. During this period when the cubs are learning to hunt, these families of tigers may kill more prey animals than they can actually eat. Such 'wasteful' killing of wild or domestic prey usually indicates the presence of cubs that are learning to hunt.

title *The Deer and the Tiger*, it generated more hard information on tiger ecology and behavior than all the previous tiger stories entombed in hundreds of hunters' tales. *The Deer and the Tiger* inspired a generation of carnivore biologists across the world, and helped to arouse widespread concern for the plight of wild tigers.

In the early 1970s, the world conservation community launched the first concrete effort to save tigers from imminent extinction. Experience from other endangered species recovery programs in the West and in Africa showed that basic biological knowledge was an essential prerequisite for establishing a sound recovery program for tigers. Such scientific research could potentially help tiger conservation in three primary ways. Firstly, it identified the basic ecological needs of tigers. Secondly, it helped establish benchmarks on what could potentially be achieved in a given ecological and social context. Thirdly, only a continuous scientific evaluation could inform conservationists whether their efforts to save tigers were succeeding or failing.

Therefore, when 'Operation Tiger' was launched by the IUCN-World Wildlife Fund combine, in alliance with the governments of tiger range countries and other partners, a long-term ecological study of tigers was recognized as a priority need.

Meanwhile, a powerful new tool known as radiotelemetry had been invented in the United States to study secretive carnivores like bears and pumas. The Smithsonian Tiger Ecology Project, supported by 'Operation Tiger', was the first long-term project that employed radiotelemetry to study tigers. Commencing work in the Royal Chitwan National Park of Nepal in 1973, American biologists John Seidensticker, Mel Sunquist, David Smith and their Nepali colleagues radiotracked more than 30 tigers through the decade that followed. Their studies were supplemented and continued by Charles McDougal, who photographed and observed tigers near baited buffalos in the same area. This landmark study provided rich

details that filled out the broad outlines of tiger ecology provided earlier by Schaller.

Later, two more long-term studies of tigers employing radiotelemetry were launched: in 1986, I commenced work on tigers in Nagarahole reserve, India, in association with Mel Sunquist from the University of Florida. After 1993, this study was enlarged to include a newer study tool called 'camera trapping', in collaboration with Jim Nichols of the U.S. Geological Survey. In this technique, self-activated cameras that are automatically triggered by tiger movements are placed along trails in the forest. This research continues in Nagarahole and several other Indian sites to this day.

In the early 1990s Dale Miquelle commenced another telemetry study of tigers in the Russian Far East in association with other American and Russian biologists. His study is also continuing. In the mid 1990s a fourth long-term telemetry study of tigers was initiated by Raghu Chundawat and colleagues in the dry forests of Panna, central India.

More recently, several short-term surveys to estimate tiger distribution and abundance have been initiated in India, Thailand, Malaysia, Nepal, Indonesia, Myanmar, Laos and Cambodia by different agencies and individuals. Among these projects, the tiger surveys sponsored by the Wildlife Conservation Society (WCS) are perhaps the most comprehensive in scope.

All these scientific studies are fundamentally different from the subjective impressions recorded by early naturalists and tiger hunters. A modern biologist begins to study tigers by asking specific questions. He, or she, then applies study methods capable of generating quantitative data to answer the original questions. Based on the results, the biologist makes objective inferences. As in all other sciences, this process of refining earlier knowledge is essentially a quest for truth with no end. As new information is gathered, old ideas are modified or even abandoned.

The methods tiger biologists use to generate reliable

information are fascinating: they are what make modern wildlife science different from good old natural history.

Studying Tiger Diet

Biologists trying to determine exactly what tigers eat have a tough problem. Animals like monkeys and deer can be watched

The tigress protects her young cubs closely.

while they feed; even predators like lions and cheetahs that live in the open savannas can be observed while hunting. However, what the secretive, forest-dwelling tiger hunts, cannot usually be directly observed. The tiger's diet has to be deduced from carefully gathered indirect evidence: remains of prey carcasses, or, worse still, from bits of bone, hooves or hair, scrupulously extracted from the awful, smelly tiger droppings that biologists know as 'scats'.

I used to search the forests in Nagarahole diligently with my trackers, to locate the remains of prey killed by tigers. The stench of rotting flesh, calls of scavenging crows, or the flight patterns of vultures homing in, all helped us to locate kills. Once I found a kill, I recorded the species, its body size and weight. By weighing a

kill it is often possible to figure out how much meat the tiger ate from it. From the eruption and wear patterns of the prey animal's teeth, I could establish its age. I also recorded any signs of disease or injuries that may have rendered the prey vulnerable.

Although prey carcasses yielded valuable details, they did not represent a true sample of all the animals that tigers in Nagarahole actually killed, because smaller kills and kills made in dense cover were less likely to be found by me. However, the scats of tigers provided an unbiased sample of whatever prey the tiger actually ate.

The fact that tigers deposited their scats along trails made it easy to routinely collect scat samples. Tiger scats are distinguished from those of other large carnivores by size and by the tracks left by tigers. In case of doubt, special chemical analyses known as bile acid assays can be used to identify the species of predator that deposited the scat. After the scats are cleaned (not an enjoyable task by any means), hair and other remains of the prey animal can be identified through comparison with known hair samples from a reference collection. Examination of the overall shape, size and color of hair with the naked eye and under a microscope can identify prey species unambiguously. Once the proportions of different prey in tiger diet were determined, data from feeding trials on captive big cats allowed me to estimate even the relative numbers of different prey species killed by tigers.

Catching Wild Tigers

Biologists who want to learn details of tiger behavior must use radiotelemetry. This involves putting a belt that carries a radiotransmitter around the tiger's neck. The transmitter must be small enough not to hinder the movements and behavior of the tiger in any way. The tiny transmitter, which is powered by a miniature lithium battery that usually keeps going for about three years, broadcasts beeps on a particular frequency.

The stripe patterns on tigers are unique, like human finger prints, and can be readily used to identify individual animals.

The transmitter and the battery are housed in a metal locket sealed in waterproof resin. Armed with a receiver and an antenna, the biologist can track the tiger by homing in on the signals from the radiocollar. However, before he can radiotrack tigers the biologist faces a formidable challenge: catching the tiger in order to fix the collar! Tigers are wary animals that do not enter traps easily. The traps strong enough to hold tigers are bulky and difficult to transport. If not handled carefully, tigers may injure themselves by charging at the steel bars of the trap.

Biologists in Russia use wire snares concealed across paths to catch tigers by their paws. Early next morning, the snared animals are located using helicopters, and then darted with a chemical sedative to immobilize them quickly. Since the densities of tigers are low and there are no other animals that might harm tigers in the Russian Far East, this method works reasonably well.

In the forests of south Asia, where animals potentially capable of killing snared tigers, such as wild elephants, rhinos, wild cattle and other tigers, are abundant, snaring techniques cannot be easily deployed. Therefore, a technique called 'beat' is sometimes used for capturing tigers in Nepal and India. This method was originally invented by Nepali hunters to shoot tigers, but now serves as a tool for researchers helping to save them.

In the 'beat' technique, the wild tiger is attracted to tethered bait – usually a buffalo. Next morning, when the unwary tiger is sleeping next to the bait after a heavy meal, a capture team consisting of three riding elephants and a dozen men reach the spot. Working quietly, about 150 yards (135 meters) away from the sleeping tiger, they quickly erect a funnel-shaped 'stockade' made of strips of white cloth strung on the bushes, surrounding the sleeping tiger. There is a 30-yard (27-meter) wide opening at the narrow mouth of the funnel. The biologist, armed with a tranquillizing gun, waits on a tree near the mouth of the stockade. The team, now riding on elephants, enters the stockade from the opposite end, and forces the tiger to move away from the kill.

The tiger could, of course, easily jump over or rip through the flimsy cloth stockade, but it doesn't. Faced with the unfamiliar white object amidst the jungle greenery, the naturally wary tiger avoids the barrier, trying to thread its way cautiously through the jungle pathways. Finally, it emerges out of the narrow exit. At this instant the waiting biologist darts the tiger with a measured dose of sedative. After about five minutes it takes effect, and the animal recovers in a couple of hours.

The sedated tiger is measured, weighed, and blood and parasite samples are collected from it for the study of disease and genetics. The animal is then fitted with the radiocollar. After the tiger recovers from the sedation and walks away into the forest, the biologist can listen to its signals and track the tiger's movements.

Radiotracking Tigers

Intricate details of tiger behavior, such as activity through the day, use of habitat, space requirements and ranging behavior can only be understood by following individual tigers continuously over months or even years. Radiotelemetry is the only tool that permits us to do this.

Radiotracking works on a simple principle. A Very High Frequency (VHF) transmitter emits signals continuously. Each collared animal sends its beeps on a different frequency, allowing biologists to track several animals at the same time. The transmitters are usually designed to send signals in the 140-160 MHz range.

The biologist listens to the radio signals using a receiver, tuned to the specific frequency of the tiger that he tracks. An antenna fixed to the receiver helps in picking up signals. There are two kinds of antennas. The first, known as Dipole antenna, can pick up signals from a relatively large area, but it does not indicate the direction from which they are coming. It can only indicate that the tiger is somewhere within range, but not exactly where it is.

The exact location of the animals is found using a directional antenna known as the Yagi antenna. This antenna can pinpoint the direction to the tiger's location, because the strongest signals are heard when the antenna faces that direction. As the biologist gets closer to the animal the signal gets louder. If he moves or faces away from it, the signal becomes weaker.

The tiger can sometimes be located by moving quickly to home in on the animal by going around in a tight circle – sometimes by even seeing it. However, because tigers stay in dense cover and move quickly over rugged terrain, it is often difficult to home in on them, so a second type of tracking known as 'triangulation' is also employed. In this technique, the biologist records the direction to the animal from his location using a compass. He then quickly moves to two or three other locations and records directions from these. When all these directions are plotted on a map later, they converge on a point, which is the estimated location of the tiger.

It is not easy to radio-track tigers physically, because they move over large areas and cover distances quite fast. Because of the need to use a sufficiently light transmitter that does not hamper the tiger, only a small battery can power it. However, the small battery must also last two to three years, because catching a tiger repeatedly to replace batteries is not easy. Thus the transmitter cannot draw heavy power, and its signals are usually rather weak. For example, in the forests of Nagarahole, I could hear the signals from my tigers only from within a few hundred yards distance.

The biologist flying in an aircraft or helicopter can increase the tracking range, but these add significantly to the costs of the study. For studying the long-distance dispersal of young tigers, aircraft radiotracking is very useful. In the Russian Far East, where biologists have to cover huge distances over roadless, inhospitable terrain, helicopters are used for tracking tigers.

Recently, radiocollars with built-in Global Positioning Systems (GPS) have been developed. In these the collar sends its own signal to several satellites overhead, which estimate the location several times a day and store the information in the collar. At preset intervals the collar sends the stored information to the receiver. Such advanced GPS radiotelemetry has recently been used on tigers for the first time, in Nepal.

However, these methods of remote radiotracking do not allow us to actually watch the tiger as it hunts or interacts with other tigers. Therefore, wherever feasible, tigers are tracked either from vehicles or on foot. In India and Nepal, trained riding elephants are also sometimes used for tracking, serving as effective all-terrain vehicles.

Counting Tigers in the Wild

Confident proclamations on 'tiger numbers' in different countries, regions and individual reserves are commonplace in popular writings on tigers and in the media. Consequently, the public responds with much joy or concern, if these reported 'tiger numbers' go up or down. However, the reality is that most of these numbers are nothing more than guesses. Worse still, some numbers are downright wrong because of the unreliable 'methods' used to generate them. Tigers' secretive nature, scarcity and extensive range make it very difficult to count them reliably. Therefore, when trying to count tigers, the available material resources, manpower, and skills have to be considered in relation to why we are trying to count tigers in the first place.

Whether on a country wide or a regional scale, it is most important to know if the areas occupied by different tiger populations are expanding or shrinking. This can be done by accurately surveying and mapping the presence or absence of

After a tiger is sedated by darting, biologists measure and weigh it. The tiger is then fitted with a radiocollar. After it recovers and walks away, the biologist can track its activity and movements using an antenna and a telemetry receiver. By carefully listening to the radio signals and pointing the antenna towards the direction in which the signals are the strongest, the biologist can pinpoint the location of the tiger.

tigers, merely using their signs such as tracks or scats. For such range mapping, it is not at all necessary to count tigers.

For purposes of routine management of individual tiger reserves, it may often be sufficient to derive a simple index that tracks the ups and downs – the relative abundance – of the tiger population. Well-designed sample surveys of tiger signs can yield indices such as number of tiger track sets encountered or number of scats seen for every 10 miles (16 km) walked by survey teams. Such indices can reflect changes in tiger numbers reasonably well, without actually counting individual tigers.

There is a strong relationship between the number of prey animals in a reserve and the number of tigers in it. Prey animals are easier to see and count than tigers. Sampling methods such as line transect surveys can be used, where observers walk along straight lines to count prey animals and measure distances at which they are detected. The distances and counts are analyzed using computer models that estimate the number of prey animals in the area, including the proportion probably missed during the survey. Once prey numbers are estimated reliably, 'ballpark' estimates of tiger numbers can be calculated from them.

However, to set management goals, to validate simpler monitoring methods or to understand tiger biology in detail, it is necessary to get accurate counts of tigers in selected sample areas. In such cases, there is no alternative to investing the necessary material resources and scientific skills. Estimates of home-range sizes of breeding tigresses derived from radiotracking provide a reasonable basis for guessing at total numbers of tigers. However, because of the huge effort and material resources needed to track even a handful of tigers, radiotelemetry is not the most efficient method for counting tigers.

Camera trapping is a new tool used for counting tigers, based on the fact that stripe patterns are unique to each individual animal, like human fingerprints are. Camera traps contain self-activated units that fire connected cameras when a tiger crosses in front of them. These traps obtain close-up photos of tigers from which the number of distinct individual tigers in the surveyed area can be counted by comparing stripes.

However, for various reasons, all the tigers in the sampled area may not be photographed, resulting in undercounts. Therefore, camera trap photography becomes a truly useful tool only when used in combination with a population estimating method known as capture-recapture sampling. This method was originally developed for counting rodents, fish and birds, after artificially tagging individuals. In the case of tigers, however, the protocol uses natural stripes rather than artificial tags.

Capture-recapture camera trapping is done on different occasions called sampling periods. Using the photographs, capture history records of all individual tigers photographed are built up. Computer models analyze how often identified tigers turned up in the different samples, to estimate the proportion of the total number of tigers in the area that were actually photographed. Thus, without actually photographing all the animals in the sampled area, reliable estimates of total tiger numbers can be obtained.

Jim Nichols and I used this method to count tigers at nine different sites in India. Our recent work suggests that, in multi-year studies, such capture-recapture sampling can also provide estimates of annual survival and recruitment rates in tiger populations. Such estimates are hard to obtain, even after radiotracking dozens of tigers over many years. It is likely that in future, DNA extracted from tiger scats or hair can be used to identify individual animals and the powerful capture-recapture estimation method can be applied to such data.

Although tigers appear quite striking in zoo enclosures, in the natural brush and grass of the forest they are well camouflaged.

How Tigers Came To Be

Evolutionary Relationships

Before we try to understand living tigers, we need to step back in time briefly, to learn how tigers originally evolved, adapted to varied habitats, spread across Asia and came to occupy their historically recorded range. The work of palaeontologists, geologists, taxonomists, geneticists and biogeographers has significantly advanced our knowledge of how tigers evolved and spread through Asia.

Taxonomists have classified all mammals, including humans, into 26 units known as 'orders'. Just as we belong to the order *Primata*, together with monkeys and apes, tigers belong to an order known as *Carnivora*. Among the *Carnivora*, tigers belong to the cat family, *Felidae*, distinct from other families like bears (*Ursidae*), dog-like animals (*Canidae*), hyenas (*Hyaenidae*), civets (*Viverridae*), mongooses (*Herpestidae*), raccoon-like animals (*Procyonidae*), and badger- and weasel-like animals (*Mustelidae*).

Within the family *Felidae*, tigers belong to a genus called *Panthera* (or roaring cats) that includes the lion, leopard, jaguar and the snow leopard, but excludes the puma. *Panthera* species are distinguished from other cats by the free-floating hyoid bones in their throat which enable them to roar loudly. Thus, in scientific nomenclature, which is used across the world (unlike common names of animals that differ from place to place), the tiger is designated by combining the names of its genus and species: *Panthera tigris*.

Traditionally, species are further split into subspecies. Initially, taxonomists came up with eight tiger subspecies: *Tigris* in southern Asia, *Altaica* in northeastern Asia, *Amoyensis* in south-central China, *Virgata* in western Asia, *Corbetti* in Indochina, and *Balica*, *Sondaica* and *Sumatrae* in the Indonesian islands of Bali, Java and Sumatra, respectively. Recent studies, however, suggest that only three among these categories may be valid, and the rest merely consequences of poor inferences made by past taxonomists.

Since the 1970s, molecular geneticists have developed methods that analyze material obtained from blood and tissue samples from wild cats and other animals to determine the degree of relatedness among species and to establish evolutionary lineages. Stephen O'Brien and his colleagues at the National Institute of Cancer in the U.S.A. have led these efforts to 'set the molecular clocks' that trace big cat ancestry. Another new biogeographic approach examines the patterns of past climate change to make ecology-based inferences about the distribution of vegetation, prey species and tigers through evolutionary time.

Modern scientists thus rely on a combination of the above approaches — morphology, genetics, biogeography and ecology — to understand the evolution, radiation and distribution of tigers from the prehistoric past into recent times.

Factors That Shaped Tiger Evolution

The tiger has been shaped by natural selection to be a master predator of ungulate prey its own size or even larger. The tiger's essential ecological needs are met if there is suitable shade and cover, sufficient prey, and adequate supplies of water. During its evolution, the big cat has spread its range by opportunistically moving in to occupy its niche as a hunter of large prey in forested regions of Asia. This radiation of tigers was driven by two primary factors: changes in climate and vegetation, which in turn led to the radiation of large ungulate prey species across Asia.

Tigers have adapted to the sub-zero winter colds and snow in the Russian Far East.

Tigers are adapted to living in the hot, dry forests of northern India.

During the Pleistocene geological epoch that began about two million years ago and lasted until the advent of the present Holocene epoch, approximately 10,000 years ago, the climate of the earth underwent periodic fluctuations. It alternated between cool-dry periods (Glacials), and warm-moist periods (Inter-glacials). It is estimated that there may have been 50 or more such cycles during the last 2.6 million years. Each of these climatic spells lasted several thousand years, giving the tiger ample time to respond to environmental changes. The latest major cold spell, known as the Last Glacial Maximum (LGM) occurred about 20,000 years ago.

During cold spells, glaciers advanced south, covering northern and central parts of Asia. Because a lot of the water on earth was frozen permanently into these glaciers, the sea levels dropped, exposing land bridges that provided a connection between mainland Asia and the adjacent islands. During these glacial periods, the climate was drier and rainfall lower. Consequently, the forested regions in Asia shrank, and grasslands expanded.

On the other hand, during the warm inter-glacial periods the ice sheets retreated and melted, raising the sea levels and submerging land connections. The wetter, warmer climate enabled forests to expand once again, pushing back the grasslands.

In response to these fluctuations in climate and vegetation, numerous forms of large ungulates such as the deer family (*Cervidae*), antelopes and cattle (*Bovidae*) and wild pigs (*Suidae*) evolved and spread throughout Asia. As ecologist Mel Sunquist and colleagues showed recently, the tiger evolved and radiated primarily as hunter of these ungulates. Adapted to preying in dense cover on large ungulates weighing up to a ton, the tiger had to be a large, solitary, stalk-and-ambush predator. As tigers spread, exploiting the rich prey base of ungulates, their range expansion was constrained by a few ecological factors.

Tigers are adept swimmers, capable of crossing water bodies as wide as 5 miles (8 km). Yet, rising sea levels and loss of land bridges appear to have halted their expansion into forested parts of Borneo, Sri Lanka and North America during the warm inter-glacial periods. Although forests generally expanded during the warm spells, in some areas of west Asia, expansion of

Water is an essential requirement of tiger habitats.

deserts may have isolated the tiger populations from their nearest neighbors in China.

During the glacial spells, land connectivity increased because sea levels dropped. However, expansion of the short-grass savannas at the expense of forested habitats favored by tigers may have been a barrier to their range expansion, particularly in southern Asia.

The historically recorded distribution of tigers, therefore, results from a complex interplay of earlier events – changes in sea levels, climate-vegetation dynamics and the eruption and range expansion of large ungulates over thousands of years. In the Holocene epoch over the last 10,000 years, in addition to these natural factors, human societies have also altered landscapes and vegetation patterns dramatically through the use of fire and farming. Consequently, in recent times humans have played a predominant role in determining where tigers have continued to live.

Timing of Evolution and Radiation

Taxonomists, geneticists and ecologists do not always agree on all the details as to where and how tigers evolved and radiated. Andrew Kitchener of the Royal Scottish Museum and his colleagues have recently synthesized available evidence, to make reasoned inferences about the evolution, classification and the biogeography of tigers. According to their synthesis, *Panthera* cats branched away from the other *Felidae* about five million years ago in Asia. Within the *Panthera* lineage, tigers originated in eastern Asia first, followed by the splitting away of the lion and leopard lineages in Africa. Fossils of big cats described as early 'tigers' that are smaller than tigers we find now in south Asia, but larger than those in Sumatra, have been found in Henan, China, and on the Island of Java. These fossils are estimated to be 1.66 to 2.0 million years old, suggesting that tigers were already widely distributed across Asia.

Fossil evidence from the subsequent periods shows tigers were widely distributed over China and Southeast Asia 1.3 to 0.7 million years ago. Tiger fossils that are 700,000 to 50,000 years old occur over an even wider region that includes Siberia, the Altai and the Caucasus in Russia. Around the same time, tigers appear to have spread into Japan as well as into Beringia, the land bridge that once connected Asia to North America. However, there is no evidence that tigers ever entered the North American continent.

Tigers may have colonized the Indian subcontinent only about 12,000 years ago. They appear to have entered the West Asian region from India through Afghanistan. However, tigers apparently failed to colonize Sri Lanka, before rising seas cut off the island from India. Another alternative scenario is that tigers were already present in India earlier, but their range shrank subsequently due to contraction of forests during the last glacial maximum 20,000 years ago. Similarly, although tigers occupied peninsular Malaysia and the Sundaic islands (Sumatra, Java, Bali) they could not colonize Borneo because of rising sea levels. The extinction of tigers in Japan appears to have been a consequence of human colonization, possibly compounded by environmental changes.

In purely geographic terms, the tiger range spanned 100° of longitude and 70° of latitude on the earth's surface. The tiger's historic range covered about 30 present-day countries: Armenia, Azerbaijan, Georgia, Iraq, Iran, Turkey, Kazakstan, Kyrgyzstan, Tajikistan, Uzbekistan, Turkmenistan and Afghanistan to the west; Mongolia, China, Russia and North and South Korea to the north; Pakistan, India, Nepal, Bhutan and Bangladesh to the south; and Myanmar, Thailand, Laos, Cambodia, Vietnam, Malaysia, Singapore and Indonesia to the east.

The present geographic range of tigers is greatly restricted as a consequence of human impacts. The tiger has been extirpated from over half the countries listed above. It now survives only in 13 of them: Russia, China, India, Nepal, Bhutan, Bangladesh, Myanmar, Thailand, Laos, Cambodia, Vietnam, Malaysia and Indonesia. Even within this shrunken range, tigers actually survive only in about 150 populations that occupy less than five per cent of their former vast domain.

Natural Habitats of Tigers

Because of their adaptability, tigers occupy a wide variety of biomes and habitats. In terms of climatic variations they tolerate temperatures as low as -31° F (-35° C) in the Russian Far East as well as the heat of 118° F (48° C) in northern India. Tigers occur in dry forests where the annual rainfall is a mere 24 in (600 mm), and in tropical evergreen forests where it may reach

Recent measurements in the field suggest that tigers in the Russian Far East are about the same size as tigers in India.

Tigers stalk their prey using every bit of available cover, to get within range for the short final rush.

395 in (10,000 mm). However, availability of free surface water, to drink regularly, appears to be crucial. Tigers simply cannot make it in some arid environments where lions and leopards thrive. Tigers' habitats can range from sea level to elevations of almost 10,000 ft (3000 meters). Occasionally they cross some mountain passes at 13,000 ft (4000 meters) in the eastern Himalayas.

In south and southeast Asia, tigers occur in tropical wet evergreen forests, semi-evergreen forests, subtropical forests, peat forests, moist deciduous forests, dry deciduous forests and dry thorn forests. They also occur in the grasslands and mangrove forests of major river deltas. In southern China, tigers survive in temperate hill forests. Tigers of the Russian Far East inhabit temperate pine-dominated forests as well as the mixed conifer-broadleaf forests. Before they were exterminated, the tigers in western and central Asia lived in habitats as varied as the reed-beds and plume grass in low lands, juniper and tamarisk forests of the hills, and even in narrow ribbons of gallery forests that snaked across inhospitable desert environments.

With the recent human modification of their natural habitats, tigers have been forced to adapt to drastically altered vegetation in some parts of their range, like plantations of timber trees, oil palm, rubber, sugarcane, cardamom and coffee.

The Prey of Tigers

Tigers do eat a variety of prey animals ranging in size from termites to elephant calves, as anecdotally documented by many naturalists. However, their evolution and survival are linked primarily to the availability of large-bodied prey, particularly ungulates weighing more than 45 lb (20 kg). In the absence of such principal prey, tigers simply cannot make it.

There are several species of principal prey in Asian forests. Although tiger diet has not been well studied over the animal's entire range, several ungulate species can be readily identified as principal prey: in northern Asia, moose, red deer, roe deer, sika deer, serow and wild pig; in western Asia roe deer, red deer and wild pig. In the subtropical and tropical habitats of south and southeast Asia, tigers have even wider choice of prey: cervids like sambar, Elds deer, swamp deer, Timorese deer, chital, hog deer and several species of muntjacs; antelopes such as nilgai and chousingha; wild cattle like gaur, banteng, kouprey, water buffalo and yak. Occasionally, they kill wild goats and goat-antelopes like nilgiri tahr, goral, serow, takin and perhaps even the recently discovered pseudo-oryx. In addition, tigers may occasionally kill Malay tapirs, and elephant and rhino calves. The most ubiquitous prey of tigers over their entire range is almost surely the wild pig. Tigers are also known to persistently hunt many kinds of monkeys and porcupines.

Occasionally tigers kill and eat other large carnivores that share their habitats, like leopards and dholes. In Russia, they are reported to prey on black bears and brown bears, and, in India and Nepal, on sloth bears. Tigers readily kill a variety of livestock – cows, buffalos, yaks, horses, camels and even domestic dogs.

The 'Subspecies Question'

Most taxonomists put all the world's tigers into one species, *Panthera tigris*. However, through natural selection pressures, tigers have had to adapt to a variety of habitats and prey types during the course of their evolution. Such local adaptations have made tigers look somewhat different in different parts of their range in terms of size, coloration and skeletal features. However, even within the same populations, individual tigers can vary greatly, confounding the larger picture of regional variations.

Traditional taxonomists treated 'different looking' tigers as different 'subspecies'; that is, the result of geographic isolation followed by separate evolution of traits in different subspecies.

In 1758, Swedish pioneer Carl Linnaeus first named the tiger *Panthera tigris*. Based on data from the Indian subcontinent, he also designated the first subspecies as *Panthera tigris tigris*. Taxonomists, who followed Linnaeus in the nineteenth and twentieth centuries, spliced off seven more subspecies of tigers.

Early taxonomists classified animals, and attributed evolutionary relationships and lineages, primarily by observing the similarities and differences in structure, known as 'phenotypic' differences. In the case of tigers, the commonly used features to discriminate 'subspecies' included measurements of the skull and other bones as well as assessments based on body size and pelage. These classifications resulted in descriptions of seven more subspecies of tigers based on perceived variations in size, skull measurements, and coloration and stripes. However, as pointed out by Andrew Kitchener, these categorizations were based on data from only 11 tiger specimens.

Because physical traits such as size and color vary greatly among individual tigers even within a region, the early subspecies classifications based on small samples of data were not dependable. However, due to widespread promotion of this 'eight subspecies' concept by conservation agencies and the international zoo community, it has taken deep root in the public mind and significantly influenced conservation decisions.

Recent evidence indicates that these putative subspecies may not be real at all. The genetic evidence suggests that about 20,000 years ago, tiger populations were interconnected, at least across mainland Asia.

Andrew Kitchener and his colleagues have recently re-evaluated the earlier subspecies classifications by re-examining tiger specimens using body size, striping patterns and skull measurements from museum specimens and old records. They synthesized this evaluation with the recent molecular-genetic and bio-geographic evidence. Their analysis suggests that the difference between tigers in different parts of their range may be 'clinal', meaning a gradual and continuous variation across Asia, rather than sharp differences arising from true sub-speciation, caused by geographical isolation and separate evolution.

Such clinal variation in tigers can be reasonably explained by established principles of zoology and ecology. Animals in the colder, northern latitudes tend to be larger because of thermal efficiency (Bergman's rule) or because of seasonal superabundance of food (Geist or Guthrie's rule). The size of prey taken can also be expected to strongly influence body size. Local climate can influence pelage coloration (Gloger's rule).

Therefore, the 'eight tiger subspecies' so dearly loved by the media and zoos may not have much of an objective basis. The alternative model of tiger evolution supported by more solid evidence seems to favor the idea that there were only three subspecies of tigers based on geographic isolation until historical times: first, the mainland Asian form *Tigris* that includes all tigers formerly split into four subspecies; second, the Sunda Island form *Sumatrae* that also included the extinct tigers of Bali and Java; third, the West Asian tiger *Virgata,* which is now totally extinct.

These findings imply that conservationists should worry less about the so-called subspecies, and think more about preserving representative samples of the wonderful variation in tiger ecology we can still observe across the range of the big cat. Understanding tigers of the past helps us to know how tigers came to be where they are now; understanding the tigers of the present will help us realize how and where tigers can live in the future.

Tigers have binocular vision enabling them to judge distances accurately.

Dressed To Kill

Body and Muscles

Among all carnivores, cats are the most exclusive meat-eaters, and tigers are the largest of all cats. Therefore, as in other *Panthera* cats and the puma, the tiger's body plan, structure and senses have all been fine-tuned during the process of natural evolution to satisfy one critical ecological need: the ability to safely subdue, kill and consume prey animals that are as large as or larger than itself.

The tiger's muscles are strong, supple and adapted for short rushes and leaps, and for grappling. The body is long and flexible, with the forequarters being markedly more muscular than the hindquarters. The tiger's head is broad and connected to the body by a thick, short neck. The hind limbs are much longer than the forelimbs. The long tail helps to provide balance during rapid motion.

The tiger's diet of meat is rich and easily digestible. Therefore, its gut is relatively short (four times the length of the body as opposed to 10 times in humans), reducing body weight. This increases the 'power to weight ratio' of the tiger, in engineering terms. The tongue is rough and well equipped for rasping meat from bones and for grooming the fur. Tigers can regurgitate the meat they have eaten, to provision their young or simply to get rid of unwanted food.

The body size of tigers has been debated endlessly in the old hunting literature. However, much of this literature is of dubious value because of the great prestige attached to hunting 'big' tigers, and the consequent subterfuges and exaggerations that tainted the hunting literature. The varied methods used for measuring dead tigers further compounded the problem. Sometimes tigers were measured from stretched skins, or with a tape held between two wooden pegs marking the tips of the nose and tail of the carcass lying prone on the ground (length 'between pegs'), or with a tape stretched along the back (length 'over curves'). In some cases, to please the dignitaries who had to shoot a 'big' tiger, their assistants used tape measures that had only 11 inches to a foot! Consequently, in the earlier hunting records from Russia and India, one finds many tigers that measured 12 to 13 feet (3.6 m) or even longer!

However, in the twentieth century, as zoological collectors and naturalists became less obsessed with killing 'big' tigers and more interested in biological accuracy, the tigers appeared to have started shrinking in the hunting literature. Also, we should note that 'record tigers' measured in zoos were often overfed, lacked exercise and were merely obese individuals unlikely to survive in the wild.

Zoologist Reginald Pocock noted that tigers were often inadequately measured and so the sizes reported in the hunting literature are often unreliable. Most biologists now measure the length of tigers along the contours of the spine, from the tip of the nose to the end of the tail. They also follow a standard method, measuring other body dimensions such as the lengths of head and body, tail, hind foot and height at the shoulder.

The typical ranges of body dimensions and weights thus recorded for tigers in India and Nepal are as follows: male tigers weigh 385 to 570 lb (175 to 260 kg) and females 220 to 385 lb (100 to 175 kg). However, because tigers can eat as much as 77 lb (35 kg) of meat at one go, the time that has elapsed since the last meal makes a substantial difference to their recorded weights. The total length of adult male tigers in south Asia is about 106 to 122 in (270 to 310 cm), and that of females 95 to

Tigers are strong, enabling them to take down prey larger than themselves.

105 in (240 to 265 cm), including a tail length of 34 to 44 in (85 to 110 cm). Height at the shoulder ranges from 36 to 44 in (90 to 110 cm).

A report compiled by V. G. Heptner and A. A. Sludski on tigers in the former Soviet Union shows that large male tigers from northern Russia were about 154 in (390 cm) long and weighed over 660 lb (300 kg). Their compilation thus indicates that the biggest Russian tigers were larger than the biggest tigers killed in Nepal and India. However, recent data on tigers captured for radiotelemetry studies in Nagarahole (India), Chitwan (Nepal) and in Sikhote-Alin (Russia) show that tigers from these three sites are all about the same size.

The tigers in Indochina and Peninsular Malaysia are smaller than Russian and South Asian tigers. The tigers surviving in the Indonesian island of Sumatra are even smaller, with adult males weighing around 220 to 310 lb (100 to 140 kg) and females only 165 to 242 lb (75 to 110 kg).

Pelage and Coloration

The primary function of the body hair of tigers (as in other mammals) is to help maintain a constant body temperature of about 99° F (37° C) by providing insulation. Tigers shed their hair once or twice a year: they have a longer coat in winter and a shorter one for the summer. As we shall see later, tigers additionally possess a special type of hair that allows them to 'feel' their surroundings. The length of body fur varies seasonally in the tigers of northern latitudes, but not in tropical areas with relatively uniform temperatures. Secretions from the skin glands on the body protect and nourish the body hair.

Although a tiger looks colorful and stands out clearly in a zoo enclosure, the tiger's stripes disrupt its outline, and help to camouflage it in the forest brush. We also have to remember that tigers' ungulate prey do not possess refined color vision.

The coat color on the head, neck, flanks, back and upper tail, varies from light tawny to deep ochre or orange. The patches around the eyes, cheeks, under-parts and inner limbs are white. The prominent white spots behind the ears are thought to assist tiger cubs to follow their mother – and each other – through tall grass.

The tiger is the only species of cat with a striped coat, all the others having spots, rosettes or blotches of various kinds. The tiger's stripes are surmised to have evolved from a primitive ancestor that possessed blotches like the ones we see on clouded leopards. The color of these stripes varies from deep brown to black, with patterns showing great individual variation. In fact, the shapes, numbers and arrangement of stripes on the tiger's body are varied enough to be used as definitive marks to identify individuals.

The coloration of tigers varies across their range: animals from tropical humid forests tend to have deeper body colors than those from cold areas or open forests. The tigers from the Indonesian islands have comparatively more stripes on their flanks.

Rarely, tigers whose pigmentation varies from the normal pattern are found. A tiger photographed in my camera traps in Nagarahole during 1993 had very scanty stripes. The pelage of a tiger recently killed by poachers in Orissa state in India was partially black, due to an overabundance of the pigment melanin.

Genetic mutations also cause the reverse phenomenon: lack of melanin, or a condition called leucism. The white tigers of the world belong to this category.

Dentition and Skeletal Structure

As ecologist John Seidensticker emphasized, the tiger's biology is essentially built around one important part of its body: the canine tooth. The ability to deliver a lethal throat bite that instantly pierces through heavy muscles of large prey, holds the key to the tiger's predatory lifestyle.

Their long, dagger-like canine teeth enable tigers to deliver the killing bite swiftly.

Chemical communication plays an important role among tigers. They leave their scent marks on trees along regular travel routes. Other passing tigers check these scent marks and leave their own scent by cheek rubbing. Tigers are able to live at very low population densities and yet communicate effectively with each other using such scent marking.

The muzzle of cats is proportionately shorter compared to that of other carnivores, enabling them to deliver a more powerful bite, but allowing space for fewer teeth. Tigers possess 30 teeth, including 6 upper and 6 lower incisors, 2 upper and 2 lower canines, 6 upper and 4 lower premolars and 2 upper and 2 lower molars. The canine teeth are 2 to 2½ in(50 to 60 mm) long on the upper jaw and 1½ to 2 in (40 to 50 mm) on the lower one.

Powerful jaw muscles inflict lethal bites using formidable, long, canine teeth set in a short muzzle. There are gaps in the jaw just behind the canines to allow these teeth to sink fully into the body of the prey. The top of the skull has a sagittal crest, a feature that provides more surface area for the attachment of the massive muscles that power the killing bite of the lower jaw. The carnassial teeth – the fourth upper premolar and the first lower molar – slice the meat while eating. The other molars and premolars are used for gripping. The somewhat blunt incisors are applied for gripping the skin of the prey while biting, and for scraping hair or meat from the kill.

The tiger's skeleton is light yet strong: a natural compromise in design between the need for lightness and agility to capture the fleet-footed but heavy prey, and the subsequent need to subdue and kill it quickly.

To provide greater leverage and power, the upper limb above the elbow must be relatively longer and strong compared to the lower limb below this joint. However, longer lower limbs confer greater speed. The tiger's limb bones above the elbow joints are long, providing increased leverage for handling heavy prey. The collarbone attached to the tiger's fore limb is much reduced in size, allowing the upper body to twist freely.

The skeletal structure permits flexing, turning, and grasping and manipulating prey with the forelimbs. The backbone is rather flexible, enabling tigers to leap and reach high speeds in short bursts. Quick running is helped by the tiger's digitigrade

(on the toes) locomotion, in contrast to our own slower, flat-footed, plantigrade walk. The long tail helps to balance the body during rapid movement. However, the tiger's short lower limb bones do not permit long-distance, high-speed running of the kind that dogs and ungulates can effortlessly turn on.

Like other cats, the tiger's feet are padded, and have five toes

A tigress sprays a scent mark on a tree.

on the front, although only four leave track impressions, and four toes on the hind feet. The toes are equipped with sharp curved claws that are extended when grasping, climbing or swatting, but remain sheathed otherwise.

Sensory Capabilities

Tigers' activity patterns are cued to hunting the prey species when the latter are most active. In recent times, tiger activity is also governed by the need to avoid human activity. Eyesight plays a very important role in the tiger's hunting technique. Tigers' eyes are sufficiently sensitive to cope with low light levels, yet they are also able to function effectively in broad daylight.

Tigers have large, round eyes with internal structures that suggest they have an excellent ability to detect movement. The retina of the tiger's eyes has an abundance of receptor cells known as 'rods', which are sensitive to low levels of light. The curvature of the lens and the presence of a reflective layer (known as *tapetum lucidum*) behind the retina also enhance the tiger's ability to see in the dark. Another type of light receptor cells, known as 'cones', are relatively less common. Therefore, compared to humans, the tiger's ability to discriminate colors and to discern details is poor.

When stalking prey, leaping and twisting and turning, tigers have to judge distances accurately and in a split-second. Such ability is also essential for moving with lightning speed through brush and thorns and safely subduing potentially dangerous prey. Tigers have forward-facing eyes, resulting in a significant overlap of images registered by both eyes. This overlap results in 'binocular vision', which we humans also possess, allowing the judgment of distances at a very fine scale.

The tiger's hearing is sharp for detecting and locating sounds in the forest. Like other cats, the tiger can probably hear sounds in the frequency range of 100-200 KHz as opposed to the maximum of 20 KHz or so that we humans can. The large external pinnae of the ear help in filtering and funneling sounds into the ear. I have often watched my radiocollared tigers hear and respond to sounds – such as prey moving through brush or people talking – at much greater distances than I could hear them.

The sense of touch is very important for tigers. The cat's padded feet allow it to feel the substrate, and avoid dry leaves, helping it walk incredibly silently for an animal of that size. The whiskers allow the tiger to 'touch' and 'feel' objects close to its forequarters. These sensitive long hairs are found on the tiger's chin, muzzle and above the eyes. The ability to 'feel' its way in total silence – even in pitch darkness, through dense cover – enables the tiger to get close to the unwary prey.

Compared to other carnivores like dogs and bears, tigers have poor smelling abilities. They use the sense of smell primarily for detecting scent from the ground or vegetation. Olfaction is apparently not very useful for tigers in locating and homing in on prey. However, a tiger's sense of smell plays a central role in its communication with other tigers.

The tiger can test 'scents' it encounters in its environment, using the Jacobson's organ which is located on the roof of its mouth. It does so through a behavior known as 'flehmen', which consists of opening the mouth with the head raised, and sticking its tongue out briefly, while the lips are curled and drawn back. The tongue is then drawn in and the strange scent tested using the Jacobson's organ. Flehmen is performed in response to scent from other tigers, other carnivore species, and sometimes with other unfamiliar odors.

Animals like tigers that depend on chemical communication must also exude scents to leave their own signals. The skin glands that secrete such special scents are elaborated and concentrated in certain regions of the tiger's body. Tigers possess scent glands around their cheeks, toes, tail and the ano-genital area. Tigers leave scent marks by rubbing these parts on trees, bushes and even on the bodies of other tigers. They also exude scents mixed with their urine and feces, leaving 'odor fields' on the ground and on vegetation, as they walk along.

When we see a tiger, we may think that it is walking 'alone', although it is leaving scent messages for other tigers almost continuously. The tiger may be solitary, but it is not alone, as we shall see later.

The long canine teeth of tigers can penetrate even the thick hide and tough muscles of large ungulate prey.

Predatory Ecology and Behavior

Activity and Thermo-regulation

Activity and movements of wild tigers are dictated by their physiological and ecological needs. These activity patterns have naturally evolved, shaped by a need to conserve energy and efficiently use the prey and other resources within the tiger's normal home range. In this chapter, we will see how the tiger actually behaves in order to meet its physiological needs: keeping cool and conserving energy. We will also examine how tigers derive nutrition from hunting, and, after the kill is made, how the tiger protects its kill from competitors while being inactive.

Tigers in the Russian Far East tolerate subzero winter colds of -31° F (-35° C), by sheltering under rocks, boulders or logs. They seem to use the aspect of mountain slopes to avoid extreme cold weather. Wherever possible they sun themselves to warm up. Having evolved in cooler environments originally, tigers are better equipped to tolerate cold than extreme heat. However, tigers do occur in some habitats where it can get very hot indeed: in reserves like Sariska and Ranthambore in northern India, daytime temperatures can shoot up to 118° F (48° C). Unlike lions, tigers are not adapted to being in direct sun for long periods in hot weather. Therefore, almost everywhere in their range, tigers are more active during the cooler parts of the day. During the hottest parts of the day they tend to lie up under dense shade. Wherever undisturbed pools or streams are available, tigers lie down in the water to cool off.

When I radiotracked tigers in Nagarahole on hot summer days, if there was a pool in the vicinity of where a tiger rested, it was almost certain that the tiger would come and lie down in the pool, at least for a few minutes. In northern India, where daytime temperatures get much higher, they appear to have an even stronger affinity to water. In reserves such as Kanha, Bandavgarh and Ranthambore tourists can often spot tigers cooling off in pools. Raghu Chundawat, radiotracking tigers in Panna reserve in central India, found that they sometimes sheltered in caverns deeper than 10 to 15 ft (3 to 5 meters) to escape from the scorching heat. He also found they did not use some prey-rich areas in summer, because of the lack of shade necessary for thermoregulation.

Tigers have to be active at times of the day when they can hunt most effectively. Because tigers hunt in densely forested habitats, they can locate prey much more effectively when the latter are active and moving. So the tiger's activity patterns tend to closely track the activities of their prey species.

Tigers can see better and detect movements under lower light levels than their ungulate prey. Therefore, with increasing darkness, tigers attain a greater ability to surprise their prey. Consequently, to avoid heat as well as look for prey in darkness, tigers are usually active from dusk and dawn.

If tigers are preying predominantly on diurnal species such as chital, hog deer and swamp deer, then they are forced to be more diurnal too. However, human activities, such as hunting and forest product collection, often force even naturally diurnal ungulates to become nocturnal. In such disturbed habitats, tigers also tend to be highly nocturnal, becoming more diurnal as disturbances are eliminated. In Ranthambore Tiger Reserve in India, during the 1980s, after intrusions of woodcutters and graziers were eliminated, sambar, chital and tigers were all observed to become more diurnal. The tigers I radiotracked in

The tiger's daily activity patterns are closely linked to those of its prey species.

Nagarahole were most active between 6.00 pm and 9.00 am: they tended to rest between 9.00 am and 3.00 pm, increasing their activity levels gradually thereafter.

Movement and Hunting Behavior

Movements of tigers are usually linked to one of the three following factors: hunting, maintaining social communication with other tigers, and avoiding the only enemy they fear – man. Here we will look at movements and ranging patterns in relation to predation, rather than from the point of view of social organization, which is examined in the next chapter.

Tigers move around within their usual home ranges while hunting. While these ranges tend to be smaller and predictable for residents, they are large and not fixed in the case of transients, as we will see later. Therefore, how far a tiger has to move while searching for prey depends on its age, sex, and social status also. The most important factor determining distances moved by a hunting tiger is the likelihood of encountering wild prey, and in some cases, domestic livestock.

How far tigers move to find prey depends on the probabilities of their encountering prey. A tiger is likely to locate its quarry earlier if there are more prey animals around in its habitat. Therefore, prey density – for example the number of deer in a square mile of forest – is a critical determinant of tiger movement rates. In Nagarahole, which is a rich area with high prey densities of 175 ungulates packed into a square mile, my radiocollared tigers moved over relatively short distances. The range of daily movements of tigers radiotracked in Chitwan and Nagarahole has been around 1 to 6 miles (2 to 11 km). They usually moved at an average rate of 220 to 750 yd (200 to 700 meters) per hour, searching the jungle slowly and lying still intermittently.

Tigers attempt to maximize their chances of finding prey by concentrating their search efforts in areas intensively used by prey. In most tiger habitats ungulate prey tend to concentrate at favored sites with an abundance of forage and water. Of the 148 tiger kills that I examined in Nagarahole, 50 per cent were within 110 yd (100 meters) of localities like water holes, grassy clearings and swamps favored by ungulate prey. Tigers killed about 45 per cent of their prey at the habitat edge between grassland and forests.

Tigers use roads, trails, and game paths in the jungle to move swiftly between areas where they actually attempt to hunt. In Nagarahole, I observed my radio-collared tigers make zigzag sweeps through trails in dense *Lantana* cover, trying to flush and ambush sambar deer. Sometimes, tigers worked the edges of grassy areas and woodlands, looking for chital and gaur that preferred to feed there. More rarely, they waited along paths likely to be taken by prey animals in anticipation of ambushing them. Just padding along, listening and looking, and then stealthily homing in on the unwary prey seems to be the tiger's primary hunting method.

Tigers hunt in fairly thick cover. Of the 148 tiger kill sites I examined in Nagarahole, about 80 per cent were in dense cover. However, tigers have to be careful while ambushing very large, potentially dangerous prey such as gaur or wild buffalo. I found that, unlike other prey, adult gaur were almost never attacked in thick cover. Errors of judgment when hunting such dangerous quarry can result in serious injuries, which eventually lead to death from starvation. Unlike an injured lion, which sometimes recovers by scavenging kills made by other members of its pride, the solitary tiger is most likely to starve to death before its injuries can heal.

Once a prey animal is located, the tiger begins the difficult task of concealing its own bulk, while at the same time moving within range for a rapid, short final rush, usually only about 50 to 100 ft (15 to 30 meters). However, in open habitats, such as the lakes of Ranthambore, tigers do charge over distances of

A tigress in the final moments of a stalk in Ranthambore reserve, India.

330 ft (100 meters) or more, coursing after sambar deer browsing aquatic plants. Such hunting behavior is not typical of tigers inhabiting denser forests.

It may take the tiger a long time to stalk within range for the final rush: several minutes or even over an hour. The tiger lowers its body profile by crouching, and moves forward

Tigers can attain high speeds, but only over short distances.

haltingly, observing the prey carefully all the time. Every bit of available cover is used: grass, brush, fallen logs — and among the tigers of Ranthambore — even tourist vehicles! When the prey lowers its head to feed, the tiger slinks forward. If the prey appears to be alert, the tiger freezes like a statue, except for the tip of its tail, which betrays all the intense excitement. Then comes the final rush.

Unlike African lions, cheetahs and hyenas, whose full hunting sequences can be easily observed, there are no data to show how many of the final rushes that a tiger makes at the prey actually succeed. Success rate is impossible to measure in forest predators, because full hunting sequences are rarely observed.

Indian naturalists Valmik Thapar and Fateh Singh Rathore, who have observed many tiger hunts in Ranthambore, guess that only ten per cent of these attempts actually succeed.

Capture, Handling and Killing of Prey

Tigers prey on a variety of hoofed animals. While handling ungulates much smaller than themselves, tigers have little cause to worry. Prey in the size range of 45 to 110 lb (20 to 50 kg) are usually knocked down and killed swiftly with a bite through the nape or skull.

However, with larger prey such as gaur, buffalo, red deer, sambar or nilgai, the tiger has to be extremely careful. The flailing hooves of such powerful ungulates can seriously injure a tiger, and their horns or antlers can inflict lethal wounds. Despite their relatively smaller size wild pigs can be particularly pugnacious adversaries to tackle. Large boars, which can weigh over 200 lb (90 kg) and sport vicious curved tusks, can even disembowel and kill a tiger that 'handles' them ineptly. With all such potentially dangerous quarry, the element of surprise that catches the prey off guard is essential to the tiger. On several occasions, I have seen herds of gaur advance in a menacing phalanx towards a tiger that failed to stalk them undetected. The element of surprise lost, the tiger invariably retreated in every instance.

Therefore, the tiger tries to surprise the prey with a final rush from the flanks or from behind the animal selected for attack. The momentum of the initial impact of the charging tiger quite often knocks the prey down. If not, the tiger tries to grasp the prey animal with its forepaws and pull it down to the ground. Even as the prey is being brought down the tiger tries to bite its throat to begin the process of strangulation. All this while the tiger must keep its own body away from the flailing hooves or horns of its victim.

After a brief struggle the prey is strangled to death by its windpipe being crushed. Less often, the prey animal is asphyxiated to death by biting on its nose. With smaller prey, the bite is often delivered to the nape and death occurs from rupture of the neck vertebrae or spinal cord. The tiger may be able to grasp and twist the neck of the collapsing prey, so that the animal's own considerable weight is used as leverage to break its neck. Sometimes, the prey dies from the rupture of major blood vessels.

The techniques described above are typically used to kill ungulate prey. Occasionally, tigers kill and eat other types of large and potentially dangerous prey. These include brown and black bears in Russia; sloth bears, leopards and dholes in southern Asia; and porcupines everywhere. Although relatively small, porcupines appear to be a dangerous prey, based on numerous reports of tigers being seriously wounded by their quills.

Prey Consumption and Killing Rates

Soon after killing, the tiger drags the carcass away and hides it in dense cover to guard it from other predators or scavengers, unless the prey is too heavy or there is no suitable cover nearby. I observed drag distances up to 380 yd (350 m) in Nagarahole, although the average was around 55 yd (50 m). The tiger normally starts feeding at the rump, and may consume 45 to 77 lb (20 to 35 kg) of meat in the first meal. Afterwards, unless it is disturbed, it rests close by, guarding the kill from other tigers and scavengers. Depending on the size of the kill, and the number of animals feeding off it, a tiger usually stays for three to five days, consuming 175 to 220 lb (80 to 100 kg) of meat, or half the weight of a sambar kill. When hungry, tigers may scavenge kills of other tigers or other predators, and eat fairly putrid meat. They also scavenge meat off animals that died from disease or other causes.

Nutritional needs of tigers vary with age, sex and body size of the animal. Adult female tigers in zoos are fed 11 to 14 lb (5 to 6 kg) of meat daily, consuming 4000 to 4400 lb (1800 to 2000 kg) of meat per year. However, wild tigers are not served dressed meat like the tigers in zoos. A significant proportion of the prey animals they kill comprises inedible or unpalatable body parts such as large bones, thick hide, skulls, horns, hooves, hair, and contents of the rumen sack, stomach or gut. These parts are either not eaten at all, or pass undigested through the gut of the tiger. The parts that are not consumed (mainly large bones, skulls with horns, parts of skin or the gut contents) weigh up to a third of the live weight of the animal. Therefore, a sambar doe that weighs 330 lb (150 kg) may provide only about 220 lb (100 kg) of consumable meat for the tiger. Wildlife biologists usually estimate the prey intake in terms of the weight of live prey needed to sustain tigers.

An adult male tiger kills about 7900 lb (3600 kg) of live prey, and an adult tigress about 6600 lb (3000 kg) every year, just to survive. Considering an average prey weight of 110 lb (50 kg) (the size of a chital doe), these tigers would have to kill about 60 to 75 prey animals per year. If the average prey weight were about 220 lb (100 kg) the tiger would have to make only about 40 to 30 kills. The average weight of prey killed by tigers was 135 lb (61 kg) in Chitwan and 198 lb (90 kg) in Nagarahole. Therefore, an average tiger must kill about 45 to 50 deer-sized prey animals every year, or one kill every seven to eight days. A tigress raising three cubs needs to kill about 60 to 70 animals or one animal every five to six days.

The kill rates estimated above are typical for prey like sambar, chital and wild pigs in the tropics where the carcasses decompose rapidly. In Chitwan and Nagarahole, tigers typically fed off their kills for three to four days. In Nagarahole, I observed that when tigers killed adult gaur that weighed 1100 to 2200 lb (500 to 1000 kg), only about 10 to 20 per cent of the meat was usually consumed, the rest being scavenged by other animals.

On the other hand, during Russian winters, when kills do not decompose rapidly as in the tropics, tigers are reported to feed for two weeks or longer. Such effective utilization of kills may significantly lower annual kill rates for large animals like red deer, moose and cattle.

Prey Selectivity

How do tigers exploit the prey base within their habitats while competing with other predators? To answer such questions, biologists have always been interested in patterns of prey selectivity. Do tigers kill randomly, killing the different types of prey roughly in the proportions they occur? Or, do tigers preferentially kill certain prey types, thereby taking other prey types less often than we expect? If tigers are indeed selective predators, do they kill their prey animals based on species, body size or some other factor that renders the prey vulnerable to predation?

It is difficult to answer these questions well, because we cannot actually observe the process of prey selection or assess how a particular prey may become vulnerable to tiger predation. However, we can estimate the numbers of different prey types in a given habitat and compare it to what the tigers are actually eating.

Although I discovered that the tigers of Nagarahole ate at least 13 different species of prey, including such rare items as elephant calves, monkeys, sloth bears, dholes, civets, porcupines and other small creatures, these prey were not really important. The principal prey of tigers in Nagarahole were five species of ungulates: gaur, sambar, chital, muntjac and wild pig. These ungulates contributed over 95 per cent of the meat consumed by tigers. Similar prey preferences have been observed in other studies.

I estimated the abundance of principal prey using line transect sample surveys and compared this to their relative abundance of occurrence in tiger diets. I found tigers preferred larger species such as gaur and sambar, and killed disproportionately more of them in comparison to the more abundant chital.

In terms of prey size, tigers of Nagarahole showed a definite preference for large prey that weighed more than 265 lb (120 kg) over medium-sized and smaller prey. In all the species killed, younger animals seemed more vulnerable to tiger predation. Chital and sambar stags appeared to be more prone to tiger predation than does, possibly because stags roamed widely and alone during the rutting season. Although tigers did take many old prey animals, they also killed others that were in their prime. When an epidemic of foot-and-mouth disease swept through Nagarahole in 1989, leaving many gaurs lame with hoof sores, tigers selectively killed them, effectively exploiting their increased vulnerability.

Man-eating Tigers

It is likely that during prehistoric times, tigers viewed human beings as normal prey. However, when our ancestors discovered the use of controlled fire, tools, agriculture and cooperative hunting, they learnt to defend themselves against tiger attacks. Like other cats, tigers are quick learners: through observation, they may soon have developed greater respect and caution for the roaming bands of people sharing their range.

In 1300, Marco Polo mentioned tigers being feared as man-eaters in China. More recently, with the advent of steel, gunpowder and firearms, humans became the aggressors, and began to harass and hunt tigers, eliminating the animals from vast parts of their range. It was at this juncture perhaps that tigers stopped viewing human beings as normal prey. Consequently, they began to avoid humans, although readily killing livestock when opportunities came up. This was the

After making a kill, a tiger drags the prey into dense cover to hide it from other tigers, competing predators and scavengers.
If undisturbed it stays with the kill for about two to three days in the case of smaller kills like this chital, and even longer with larger kills.

Although tigers are generally solitary, they do associate with each other occasionally.
Sometimes they even share kills, particularly if they are related animals.

normal behavior of wild tigers, recorded over the last two to three centuries.

However, aberrant individual tigers that attacked human beings, because of hunger, inexperience, and injuries or in defense of cubs, have always existed. Such occasional manslaughter does not necessarily lead to persistent man-eating behavior, but there is no doubt that some tigers that accidentally discover human vulnerability, later become man-eaters.

In the nineteenth and earlier part of the twentieth century there were many reports of man-eating tigers from different parts of their range in Asia. Man-eating tigers terrorized entire regions and killed many people. Historically, the most persistent reports of serious man-eating came from Russia, southern China, Singapore and parts of India. At the beginning of the nineteenth century, man-eating tigers rendered parts of India almost uninhabitable. Tigers killed 200 to 300 people per year in the same period, when the present-day bustling city-state of Singapore was being settled. Later in the nineteenth century, marauding tigers caused weekly markets to shut down over a distance of 90 miles (150 km) in Manchuria. Cossack guards had to be employed to protect Chinese coolies working on a railway project there. Sixty people were killed in a single village in central China within one week in 1922.

The problem of man-eating tigers was persistent and endemic in Bengal, Central Provinces and the Himalayan foothills of India, well into the twentienth century. The most famous of these man-eaters were the ones hunted and described in chilling detail by naturalist Jim Corbett. The Champawat tigress that Corbett managed to shoot after four years of tenacious effort had reportedly killed 236 people during her reign of terror in the Kumaon area between 1907 and 1911.

Historically, man-eaters have not been a major problem in Indochina, Malaysia, Indonesia and southern India. Indeed, a satisfactory ecological explanation does not exist for the pattern of man-eating observed in Asia during the past two centuries. Perhaps man-eating behavior gets established from the complex interplay of several ecological and social factors: the numbers of tigers, natural prey availability, topography and hunter accessibility, amount of interface between human settlements and tiger habitats, human density, local tradition of tiger hunting, potential for quick retaliation and sheer chance.

In areas such as the Sundarban mangrove forests in India and Bangladesh, even now, tigers kill dozens of people every year. Most victims are local fishermen, honey hunters and woodcutters. Sundarban man-eaters may not be merely aberrant individuals; they may comprise a substantial proportion of the tiger population. These tigers appear to opportunistically hunt down humans, just as they would hunt chital, pigs or macaques in this incredibly inhospitable riparian delta.

The relationship that prevails between tigers and humans in Sundarban is unique in this world. It is a remnant of the more 'natural' relationship that probably existed before technology enabled humans to win their psychological war over tigers, through harassment, intimidation and persistent hunting. This natural relationship has probably been preserved because the inhospitable terrain of Sundarban made it more difficult for humans to wage a successful war of intimidation on tigers than in other parts of their range.

Competition and Coexistence with Other Predators

Over much of their range, tigers share their habitats with other large carnivores. Many of these, such as the four Asian bear species and the striped hyena, are not true predators that regularly compete with tigers for their prey. However, other carnivores like the leopard, dhole, wolf and lion can directly compete with tigers over a common prey base in many parts of the tiger's range.

Tigers are much larger (330 to 550 lb / 150 to 250 kg) than leopards (88 to 155 lb / 40 to 70 kg), and wolves or dholes (33 to 55 lb / 15 to 25 kg). They can generally be expected to be more dominant in encounters, although the pack-hunting behavior of the latter two species may neutralize this advantage.

Reliable data are scarce on interactions between tigers and dholes. I have, however, observed a pack of hunting dholes apparently avoiding a resting radiocollared tiger. In another instance at Nagarahole, the naturalist K. M. Chinnappa observed a tigress with a cub appropriating a kill from a pack of dholes, and killing two dogs in the process. Apparently dholes are occasionally killed and eaten by tigers (and leopards) in Nagarahole based on the evidence of dhole hair found in the scats of these felids.

Leopards are clearly socially dominated by tigers, and excluded from prime tiger areas as reported from Chitwan and Kanha meadows. In Nagarahole, I have observed tigers chase leopards up trees. There are many natural history accounts of leopards being killed and even eaten by tigers. However, diet data from several sites where both these big cats occur shows up a very interesting pattern of competition and coexistence between tigers and leopards. During the early 1980s in the forests of Huai Ka Khaeng in Thailand, where large prey species such as banteng, gaur and sambar had been virtually eliminated by human hunters, leopards did much better than tigers, by surviving on small prey like muntjac. In Chitwan and in the meadows of Kanha, where large prey is scarce compared to the super-abundant chital, tigers and leopards compete for the same prey base. Here, tigers appear to exclude leopards from prime areas through behavioral dominance.

In Nagarahole, however, both large and medium-size prey are abundant. Here tigers and leopards selected different size classes of prey, and, consequently, both the cats coexist at high densities. My radiotelemetry studies in Nagarahole showed that all three predators – the tiger, leopard and dhole – ranged over the same habitat. In the African savannahs the open terrain favors mutual avoidance through spatial separation among lions, hyenas, cheetahs and leopards. However, in the closed forests of Asia, as long as prey of all sizes are abundant, tigers and their competitors appear to be able to share the same habitats.

Tigers and wolves share their range in parts of central and southern Asia. The wolves in southern Asia are small, and live in open areas avoided by tigers. However, even in parts of Russia and China, where wolves are larger and inhabit forests, there are no reliable data on interactions between the two species.

A part of the lion's former range in West Asia and India is too dry and hot for tigers to survive. In other parts, particularly in northern India, where the two cats overlapped, tigers may have restricted themselves to denser forests for reasons of thermo-regulation and effective hunting. There are no records of interactions between tigers and lions in the wild. Although tigers tend to be slightly larger than lions, the latter move in groups of two or more individuals. Therefore, in any chance encounters, lions are likely to be dominant over single tigers.

Originally lions occupied the open country favored for agriculture by human settlers. Lions are also diurnal, highly vocal and live in prides with fixed territories. It is likely that lions came into direct competition with the arriving human settlers. The settlers could also hunt them more easily because of their habitat preferences and behavior. Thus the early elimination of the lion by human hunters in India – even before the advent of the colonial era – may have created ecological opportunities for tigers to expand their range.

A tiger takes its own picture by tripping a camera-trap placed on its path.

Solitary, But Not Alone

Communication Among Tigers

Although tigers are solitary animals, they have a complex society of their own. In this chapter, we look at how their social organization works. Although tigers live at low densities, dispersed over extensive landscapes, they manage to keep in touch with each other regularly. In the Russian Far East, a forested area the size of New York City may harbor only half a dozen tigers. In a similar situation, six human beings will not even be able find each other, let alone form a society and maintain it. Yet, tigers do establish and maintain home ranges, find mates, and raise cubs that in turn disperse and establish home ranges of their own.

Unlike social carnivores such as lions and wild dogs, tigers do not normally move around with other tigers in groups. Therefore, they cannot keep in constant touch visually. Because tigers live in dense forests, even when they associate with each other – as in the case of a tigress raising cubs – they often cannot see each other. Consequently, they have evolved an array of communication methods: scent deposits or other signs that mark their presence and passage. Tigers also employ a variety of vocalizations – roars, moans, growls and grunts – to keep in touch with each other.

As we saw earlier, tigers are equipped with an elaborate array of scent glands located in different parts of their bodies. As they walk through the forest they continually leave scent deposits on the ground from the glands located under their feet. They also rub their cheeks against bushes or trees, leaving some scent. Sometimes tigers lie down and roll on the grass or dust, leaving some scent from their bodies on the ground.

Both male and female tigers spray scent. As they walk along forest paths (or in a zoo enclosure), tigers frequently stop, back up against tree trunks, fallen logs or bushes, lift their tails and squirt a fine misty spray of urine and scent. The viscous white liquid deposits on the target and solidifies in place, emitting scent signals for several days thereafter. With some experience, even human beings can detect this scent.

The most that we can infer from the scent mark is that a tiger has come through sometime earlier, but to another tiger, the scent probably conveys much information about the tiger that left the sign: individual identity, time since passage, sexual receptivity and reproductive condition. In a sense, each scent mark is like a detailed email message!

Tigers leave scent on the ground when they deposit their scats which are frequently combined with urine. Tigers often scrape the ground with their hind feet while they defecate, covering the scat deposit lightly with leaves and earth, probably to preserve the moisture and the scent in the scat for longer periods. Scraping also creates a prominent, easily seen patch of bare soil, drawing attention to the scent deposit.

Tigers occasionally rear up on their hind legs, using their front paws to rake claw marks on tree trunks. Sometimes they roll on the ground, churning up patterns in the dust or flattening the grass all around. All these marks serve as visual signs for other passing tigers.

Tigers also vocalize. They possess a wide repertoire of calls: loud roars that carry as far as 3 miles (5 km) through the forest in the silence of the night. Such long-distance roars are used both by female tigers in estrus and males searching for them. A tigress trying to stay in touch with her cubs also roars. If they are young cubs and the tigress does not want to draw the

Like most other cat species, tigers are solitary hunters.

attention of potential enemies to them, she emits low moans or groans. Although I have never heard it myself, many old hunters describe a tiger vocalization that sounds like the call of a sambar.

When they are at close quarters, tigers continue to signal to one another using facial expressions, body language and, for want of a better word, tail language! The facial grimaces, the position of the ears, the narrowing or widening of the eyes, in different combinations, can indicate offensive threat, defensive threat, submission, playfulness and curiosity or other responses. When cubs follow the mother in tall grass, the prominent mirror-like spots on the back of her erect ears help them to follow her.

A tiger that encounters any one of these numerous chemical, auditory or visual signals can respond by either precipitating an encounter, as in the case of a tigress in search of a mate or its cubs, or avoid an encounter, as would a young tiger passing through the home range of a resident male. David Smith, who studied tiger communication mechanisms in Chitwan, concluded that tigers signaled more intensively at the boundaries of their ranges than they did in the interior areas.

This complex communication system allows tigers to maintain contact but substantially reduces the chances of sudden encounters that could have fatal consequences for one or both the animals. The functioning of the complex social system of tigers depends primarily on this communication system.

Mating and Conception

Tigresses become sexually mature and capable of conceiving around two to three years of age. Male tigers are also probably capable of mating by this age, but are rarely able to do so in the wild because of the presence of larger, older male consorts near females in estrus.

Although captive tigers sometimes mate even when the female is not in heat, most wild tigers mate only when the female comes into estrus. Records from some western zoos indicate that estrus occurs once in 50 days or so. However, Indian zoo records and observations by Mel Sunquist and David Smith of radiocollared tigers in Chitwan, suggest a shorter estrus cycle of about three weeks. The period of heat is reported to last anywhere from two to six days.

The mating is not a strongly seasonal activity in tropical areas. Most hunters in India suggest that the peak of breeding activity occurs in the cool season. On the other hand I observed breeding activity throughout the year among my radiocollared tigers in Nagarahole, where a radiocollared tigress was observed mating in January, March, May, July and October. However, in regions where climatic conditions fluctuate greatly, as in the Russian Far East, the influence of the seasons on breeding activity may be more pronounced.

A tigress in estrus and a male tiger find each other by following scent marks and through regular bouts of roaring. They usually associate for two to three days, during which period they mate with an amazing frequency of over fifty times a day. Each copulation lasts only 15 seconds. During copulation, the female crouches stretched on the ground, while the male mounts her from behind, gripping the skin on her nape lightly with his teeth. The baculum, or penis bone, is said to stimulate the female during copulation, which assists in inducing ovulation. The courting pair indulge in much rough play, mock aggression and vocalization. To human eyes, they appear more like fighters engaged in a title bout than like lovers courting each other.

Gestation, Birth of Cubs and Early Maternity

The normal period of gestation for a tigress is 103 to110 days. As the parturition date approaches, the movement and range of the tigress becomes restricted. She must now choose a secluded spot to give birth to her cubs. Experienced tigresses choose these spots carefully: under fallen logs, in rocky crevices or in

Tigers indulge in a lot of rough play and mock aggression during mating.

*A tigress keeps her cubs at a safe location for the first couple of months.
She feeds them periodically and guards them zealously against intruders.*

thick cover, where the cubs will be safe from other predators. The litter size at birth varies from one to seven cubs with three to four cubs being the normal litter size in most productive areas. The entire litter is delivered over a period of ten hours or so. At birth, the sex ratio of cubs is equal: averaged over many litters an equal number of male and female cubs are born.

The cubs are born blind and helpless. The tigress defends them from any intruders with great ferocity and nurses them carefully. Very rarely, through temporary hormonal imbalance, a tigress may kill and even eat her cubs. The tigress hides her cubs from other predators like leopards, dholes, wolves and bears — and from other tigers. She nurses them on her milk for the first two months. If disturbed, the tigress moves them to a new hideout by carrying them in her mouth. Because the tigress has to nurse and guard her cubs, her movements become restricted, and her home range may shrink to a fraction of its usual size. David Smith found that tigresses were at their dens with cubs most of time: during the first month a tigress was never more than three-quarters of a mile (1.4 km) from her cubs.

This is a time of great risk for tiger cubs. While their mother is away hunting, her cubs may be found and killed by other predators; they may succumb to forest fires or floods that arrive suddenly. If accidentally found by people, they are usually killed.

After two months or so, the cubs start accompanying their mother. Her range once again expands as the cubs move away from the den-site with the tigress. After making a kill, she takes the cubs to feed on it. When accompanying their mother, the cubs may encounter strange tigers or other dangerous animals like elephants and rhinos. Their aggressive mother is the cubs' only defence. A radiocollared tigress in Chitwan seriously mauled biologist Kirti Tamang, who got too close to her cubs. Another tigress in Ranthambore was actually brave enough to attack and kill an intruding male tiger that got too close.

Normally, the male that sired the cubs does not attack them;

he may even share a kill amicably with the tigress and her cubs. However, other males, particularly new males that have taken over their ranges by vanquishing the father of the cubs, almost invariably attack and kill the cubs. Such infanticide has been reported from many Indian nature reserves. I saw several cases in Nagarahole, involving cubs ranging in age from three to nine months. Against a really powerful male, the mother usually has no chance of defending her cubs.

Infanticidal behavior is found in many other mammal species too. It increases the chances of the new male's offspring, rather than those of his predecessor, making it to the next generation. The female accompanied by young cubs will neither come into estrous nor mate with a new male. She is ready to mate again only when her cubs are gone. Through the evolutionary advantage it confers on practitioners, infanticide has become an established behavior in tiger social organization.

Cubs are at great risk from strange male tigers, other large carnivores, and calamities such as forest fires and floods. Therefore, even in protected habitats with plenty of prey, usually about a third of the cubs perish in the first year. In prey-scarce areas and where human intrusions are heavy, very few cubs make it through the first year to become juveniles.

Relationship Between Mother and Young

Initially the cubs are taken by their mother to the carcass, after she has made the kill alone. She may even help the cubs to open the carcass by disembowelling it first. Within a year the cubs accompany their mother most of the time, staying within a couple of hundred yards of her. They can instinctively stalk prey, and develop agility and hunting skills through a lot of play and mock aggression, among themselves and with their mother. However, they still have to learn the nuances of hunting potentially dangerous prey, which they do gradually from their mother through observation and practice.

Strong permanent canine teeth begin to emerge and replace the weaker milk teeth when the juvenile tigers are about 12 to 18 months old. Thereafter, they are potentially capable of killing large and tough ungulate prey. In Nagarahole, juvenile tigers that I estimated to be 15 months old joined their mother in killing adult gaur. Among them, at least one juvenile had lost an eye, probably through an inept attempt at catching a porcupine.

By the age of 18 months, the tiger cubs move around on their own. Although occasionally they may share a kill with their mother, they are now able to kill prey independently. However, they may stay closer to each other, rather than to their mother. The cubs still move around within the mother's home range, which is known as their natal range. Their fidelity to and association with this range is termed phiolopatry.

Between 18 and 24 months of age, the association of cubs with their mother' range gradually decreases. This is also the time when the tigress comes into estrus, mates again, and drops her next litter. Thereafter, she turns aggressive towards her older cubs, and tries to drive them away. At this stage, the cubs disperse from their natal range and attempt to establish their own home ranges.

Dispersal and Land Tenure Patterns

The timing of dispersal of young tigers is influenced by the cubs from their mother's next litter beginning to move with her. As her range expands, the tigress encounters her older offspring, and evicts them from her range by attacking them. Her older cubs disperse in response, and may move back and forth through the large blocks of habitat that include their natal range and surrounding areas. They explore their habitats, get to know good hunting spots and learn about the risks they face. The dispersing tigers, about 18 to 24 months old, look almost like adult tigers. They become transient floaters.

Sometimes male transients establish temporary, post-dispersal home ranges. However they are constantly on the move, looking for ranges of older resident males that they can take over. Usually transient tigers are not big and strong enough to take over such ranges until they are about four years or older. During this period, they often get into fights with resident tigers and with other transients.

Male tigers disperse farther than females do, usually being forced to establish post-dispersal ranges in poor habitats. Two transient males that I radiotracked in Nagarahole had ranges of over 30 to 35 sq miles (80 to 90 sq km), but in prime habitats. However, seven out of the ten male tigers radiocollared by David Smith in Chitwan were forced to settle outside the prime riparian habitats. Dispersing male tigers may move over hundreds of miles while trying to settle down. Some floaters lose their bearings, cross unsuitable terrain, and turn up in the most unexpected places. In a few cases in India, such wanderers have even jumped into enclosures to join captive tigers!

Russian zoologist Vladimir Heptner recorded instances of tigers following migrating herds of wild boar, over 600 miles (1000 km). Whether these tigers were dispersing animals that simply followed strips of riparian gallery forests is uncertain. In other parts of their range transient tigers do not 'migrate' in this manner.

Dispersing tigresses commonly try to establish home ranges next to their mother. Unless the density of resident tigresses in a neighborhood is high, female transients normally do not move far away. In some cases, the mother gradually shrinks or shifts her own territory to make room for one of her daughters. In other cases, young tigresses may try to take over a neighboring female's range by evicting her. This pattern of female home range 'inheritance' creates neighborhoods of related tigresses across the landscape. Although less frequently than among male tigers, fights do break out between resident and transient female tigers.

The behavior of transient males that disperse over great

The cubs start accompanying their mother to her kills after they are about two months old.

By the age of about six months, tiger cubs are already larger than adult leopards.

distances away from their natal ranges may be a natural mechanism that tigers have evolved to reduce probabilities of inbreeding caused by closely related females settling next to each other.

The period of transience is a very risky part of a tiger's life. Transient tigers perish in large numbers. Being smaller and less skilled than the resident adults they encounter, they often lose fights. Although tigers have remarkable ability to recover from injuries, many transients that lose fights die later. Deaths may result from the wounds, or more commonly after a period of starvation and septicemia. I once found a two-year-old tigress in Nagarahole that had died in such a fight: the necropsy yielded a broken-off canine tooth from another tiger, lodged deeply within her shoulder. Just a month earlier I had found another grievously wounded young male tiger lying next to a pond, too weak to move from hunger and his gangrenous wounds: he died the next day.

Transient tigers are also at risk from dispersing out into human settlements and get stranded in these hostile landscapes. Such tigers often end up killing livestock: they are quickly branded as 'problem tigers' and eliminated through poisoning or shooting.

Home Range and Territoriality

In this book, I have used the term 'home range' to mean the area normally used by a tiger over a relatively long period. On the other hand, the term 'territory' is used in the sense of a home range which may be defended actively against intrusion of other tigers.

The use of space by tigers appears to vary quite a bit. Given the wide variety of environments in which the animal lives, this variability is not surprising. When George Schaller observed tigers in Kanha during the 1960s, he found overlap between ranges of tigresses. The subsequent long-term radiotelemetry studies in Chitwan by Mel Sunquist and David Smith suggested that ranges of resident females were mutually exclusive: these ranges were, in fact, territories. On the other hand, studies by Dale Miquelle and his Russian colleagues that also relied on radiotelemetry revealed partially overlapping female ranges. My own work on tigers in Nagarahole shows that while female ranges are separate, there is a substantial degree of overlap between ranges. The same pattern is being observed now in Panna by Raghu Chundawat.

In Chitwan the resident male tigers appeared to occupy large territories that encompassed those of several females. The territories appeared to be non-overlapping among adult males. The number of female territories covered by a male ranged from two to seven, with three females per male being fairly typical. In the Russian Far East, males do not appear to maintain such non-overlapping ranges. In Nagarahole, camera trapping and telemetry data show that several large males operated over the ranges of resident females, with substantial overlaps. Which among these big males were 'residents', and which were 'transients', was not easy to tell. A radiocollared resident female was mating with at least two different large males in Nagarahole around the same time.

It is likely that spatial patterns in which tiger ranges are laid out in a particular landscape are determined by several factors that include prey abundance, size and shapes of the ranges and overall tiger density in the region.

How do tigers use their home ranges? They cover as much of the area as possible, as frequently as they can, using regular travel routes. While doing so they are constantly checking for scent and visual evidence of other tigers. They also continually mark their own presence through scent sprays, scrapes and vocalizations. For the most part, fights and overt aggressive encounters are avoided: ranges are defended largely by means of constant presence and marking. This behavior makes sense in terms of survival because frequent aggressive encounters would seriously incapacitate most of the tigers involved. However, when both animals refuse to yield, serious fights do break out between two tigers in defence of kills, cubs, home ranges and mating opportunities.

I had the opportunity to observe the results of several such fights between tigers in Nagarahole during the 1990s. One common fighting tactic appears to be biting the shoulder or back, trying to inflict a paralyzing bite. Several animals had such shoulder injuries in Nagarahole: some died, but amazingly others recovered. T-04, a male tiger I studied in Nagarahole, had a huge shoulder wound, which healed leaving prominent scars. But he survived and maintained his dominant status for three years afterwards. Another big male, T-117, had an ear bitten off, and developed a limp, but still held on for more than two years thereafter. Bites on hind and forelegs were also common results of such fights. In the case of cubs or juveniles killed by adult males, a bite through the skull was commonly employed.

However, we should note that tiger social organization is characterized not just by avoidance or aggression between individuals; tigers do associate with each other under the right circumstances. We have already learnt about the two-year association between a mother and her cubs, and the frequent but short associations between mating tigers. Siblings often remain associated for a few months even after they become independent of their mother. Such associations between sub-adult tigers have been observed in Chitwan, Ranthambore and Panna. In Nagarahole, I once radiotracked two transient male tigers, T-03 and T-04, and found them resting in the same large thicket. I do not know whether they were related animals. David Smith observed several of his study animals – siblings of the same sex from several different litters – associating with each other and even sharing kills. In Panna, Raghu Chundawat

observed two radiocollared females from the same litter disperse, form a coalition, and take over the range of a neighboring resident female.

Even larger associations – 'gatherings' of seven or eight tigers – have been observed around kills in Kanha and Ranthambore. In Nagarahole, during February 1989, I observed six tigers close to a sambar kill: a large male, two adult females, and three pre-dispersal juveniles. It is likely that such large temporary associations consist of two neighboring resident tigresses – possibly a mother and her daughter – sharing a kill, with their cubs, joined by the resident male that sired the cubs. However, these associations are not comparable to permanent prides formed by lions, or socially stable groups formed by other social carnivores like spotted hyenas or wild dogs.

The tiger is a predator that evolved in dense forested habitats to hunt down prey that provides several meals for itself, and possibly for its progeny. Living in a group would mean getting less meat from each kill. Moreover, group hunting does not confer any advantage in thick cover to a stalk-and-ambush predator like the tiger, unlike in savannahs where prey can be observed from a long distance, and stalked cooperatively. Most of the tiger's hunting is done in a short, sudden rush, with little opportunity to cooperate.

Belonging to a group is helpful in defending a kill from other predators in open savannahs where a carcass is highly visible to competing predators and scavengers. In dense forests, hiding the kill is an easier option. Therefore, there is no evolutionary advantage to tigers through living in groups, either for making a kill or for defending it. Consequently, tigers have evolved to be solitary rather than group-living hunters. Yet they have evolved a complex social system that suits their ecological needs perfectly. Tigers may be solitary, but they are not alone.

Although popular with some zoos, white tigers have no conservation significance.

How Many Tigers?

Tiger Numbers and Prey Availability

'How many tigers are there in your park (or state, or country, or the world)?' is perhaps the most common question that biologists or reserve managers are asked. It is almost impossible to answer this simple question accurately. We usually don't know the answer, because tigers are very difficult animals to count. Because the key to understanding how tiger populations work lies in overcoming these difficulties, in the second chapter I explained briefly the different methods used to estimate tiger numbers.

However, regardless of the methods used to count tigers, we need to understand the basic factors that determine the number of tigers in an area. This chapter examines factors that set tiger numbers at a place and drive changes in these numbers over time. Among these, available prey resources are, of course, a key external factor. There are other factors internal to the tiger population: numbers of cubs produced (fecundity), the proportion of tigers that survive each year (survival), and connectivity and movement among tiger populations.

Just as the number of cats we can rear in an apartment depends on how much cat food we can afford to buy for them, the number of wild tigers that can possibly live in a forest reserve is determined largely by how many prey animals there are in it. Of course, other factors – hunting of tigers and human disturbance for example – also have a bearing on tiger numbers. However, the natural limit on how many tigers there can be in a particular habitat is determined largely by prey abundance. This limit can broadly be termed the 'carrying capacity' of that habitat to support wild tigers.

Animal numbers are usually expressed as population density, the number of individual animals in a unit area – for example, the number of tigers per 100 sq miles (260 sq km) In this book I use the terms 'tiger density' and 'prey density' in this sense.

Tigers sometimes do eat small prey such as crabs, fish, frogs, reptiles, game birds and rodents. However, even if there is an abundance of such prey, tigers cannot survive on these, unless larger prey like deer, pig or cattle are present. This is because of energetic efficiency involved in predation; the amount of energy that a tiger has to expend to catch and eat sufficient numbers of small prey would be far greater than the energy it can derive from such prey. For example, energetically it would be impossible for a tiger to survive, if instead of catching a 100 lb (50 kg) deer every week the cat had to catch 5000 frogs. Therefore, although insects and other small prey are locally abundant, and their total biomass (living weight) exceeds that of large ungulates, they cannot substitute for the latter on the tiger's menu.

A single tiger has to kill and eat about one deer-sized prey animal, every week, just to survive through a full year. For a population of tigers to sustain itself in the long run, they have to crop their prey base in a sustained manner without depleting the stock altogether. The carrying capacity for tigers in an area is thus determined not by the total number of prey animals available, but by the annual surplus that can be killed without depleting the prey base. In a sense, cropping of the prey base by tigers is similar to a person living off the annual interest without exhausting the capital that earns it.

Of course, this pattern of 'prudent predation' exists in nature not because the tiger consciously makes a 'decision' to live off the 'income' like the human investor in the above example. Such a 'balance' between the densities of predators and prey species

It is difficult to count tigers because of their scarcity, and also because they are naturally secretive.

results from forces of natural selection that operate on an evolutionary time scale.

Given that most ungulates reproduce only one or two young per year, prey species may produce annual surpluses of about ten to 20 per cent However, factors such as disease, bad weather, competing predators and human hunters take away a part of this yearly surplus, leaving only a proportion of it available for tigers to crop. Based on the tiger studies in Kanha, Chitwan and Nagarahole, we can estimate that tigers annually crop about eight to ten per cent of the available prey biomass (standing live weight of all prey in the area) in productive habitats. In such protected areas, the tiger has a 'first claim' compared to other predators on the prey base, so to speak. Therefore, tiger densities can be close to carrying capacities in such habitats if disease, bad weather and human hunters are not major killers of prey.

To sum up, in a tiger population that survives by cropping ten per cent of the prey base annually, a prey population of 500 animals is required to provide the 50 animals required by a single tiger. Assuming that the habitat supports 150 prey animals per square mile (50 per sq km), as many protected forests in southern Asia can, this requirement would translate into an area of 3.3 sq miles (10 sq km) of land to support just one tiger. In an area where there are only 15 prey animals per square mile (5 per sq km), the extent of habitat required to support a single tiger would be about 33 square miles (100 sq km).

I was able to estimate densities of tigers using camera traps, and densities of prey species using line transect surveys, in several protected habitats of India. In reserves with high densities of ungulate prey (155 to 207 animals per sq mile / 60 to 80 animals per sq km), such as Kaziranga, Bandipur, Nagarahole, Kanha and Ranthambore, tiger densities ranged from 21 to 44 per 100 sq miles, (8 to 17 per 100 sq km), excluding small cubs. At other sites, where prey densities were lower due to ecological reasons

or human hunters, tiger densities dropped to 5 to 8 per 100 sq miles (2 to 3 per 100 sq km).

Does this mean that if prey densities keep on increasing – let us say through artificial stocking or habitat manipulations – tiger numbers can keep increasing? No. Remember that tigers have strong social spacing mechanisms. There are limits beyond

Tigers can move through grasslands without leaving any tracks.

which we cannot pack more tigers into any area, even if the prey densities increase. In good habitats, such as the grasslands of Kaziranga, tiger densities, including those of cubs, can go up to 50 tigers per 100 sq miles (20 per 100 sq km); this figure may be close to the upper limit of tiger densities that we can expect anywhere in the world.

Data from low tiger density sites are scarce: radiotelemetry-based estimates from the Russian Far East suggest that 1.3 to 2.6 tigers per 100 sq miles (0.5 to 1 tiger per 100 sq km) may be the lower limit for tiger densities. Probably at densities lower than these, tigers may not be able to communicate effectively, maintain social contacts or breed in a sustained manner. However, transient tigers may still occasionally pass through such poor habitats and survive briefly, without being able to reproduce.

Productivity of Tiger Populations

High tiger densities attained in good habitats are primarily due to the small female home ranges in such areas. Because there is

A tigress usually has three cubs every two or three years.

more prey to go around in every square mile of the forest, tigresses are able to raise cubs within smaller ranges. In other words, more females can pack into an area of a given size, at higher prey densities. Long-term observations in reserves like Panna, Chitwan and Nagarahole indicate that as prey densities increase in response to better protection, tigresses yield parts of their ranges to their daughters, increasing the number of breeding females. However, there is a limit to the number of breeding females determined by prey densities. Female ranges appear to shrink in size to a minimum of about 4 sq miles (10 sq km) or so, but no further, even in productive habitats in southern Asia. In the Russian Far East, female ranges are of 75 to 200 sq miles (200 to 500 sq km); the dry forests

of Panna in Central India have intermediate-size female ranges of 12 to 20 sq miles (30 to 50 sq km).

Prey-rich habitats can also support a higher number of transient sub-adult tigers. More cubs born are likely to survive in them than in prey-scarce habitats. As a result of all these differences, overall tiger densities can be substantially higher, by as much as 30 times in productive well-protected habitats.

In other words, if it takes an area the size of New York City to sustain 25 tigers in the deciduous forests and grasslands of southern Asia, it would take an area the size of entire New York State to support the same numbers in the Russian taiga. High-density tiger populations will naturally have more breeding females, and produce more cubs, of which a greater proportion will survive to adulthood. Thus the overall productivity of these tiger populations will be much higher than in prey-scarce habitats.

Data from long-term studies in protected habitats such as Chitwan and Nagarahole suggest that adult female tigers manage to establish ranges and start producing cubs when three to four years old. Unless her cubs die, the tigress will not breed again for the next two years or so. Normally a resident tigress appears to hold on to her range for the next six to eight years, or until she is about 10 to 12 years old. During this period she produces about three to four litters, or about 12 cubs, assuming an average litter size of three. There is a record of a tigress in Bandavgarh reserve in India surviving to an age of about 15 years.

However, the higher the density of tigers in an area, the greater is the competition for breeding ranges, and the shorter the average tenure of resident tigresses is likely to be.

Mortalities and Survival Rates

Given high cub productivity, the numbers of tigers in any given area would rapidly attain saturation densities. However, wild tigers have high natural mortality rates too. In the first year of life cubs face many threats: fire, floods, disease, humans, other predators, and infanticide by adult male tigers. The most important mortality factor (except in a few prey-rich protected areas) is probably starvation caused by the mother's failure to hunt sufficient prey, at regular intervals, within her home range. Based on radiotelemetry studies in Chitwan, tiger cubs appear to have mortality rates of 35 to 45 per cent in their first year, even in productive habitats.

During the second year of their lives, the somewhat larger juvenile tigers are relatively safe from threats posed by adverse climatic factors and predation. However, their increased nutritional requirements make starvation an ever-present threat. The second-year mortality rate may be lower, with only about 10 to 15 per cent of juveniles perishing.

The tigers that survive through their second year disperse away from their natal ranges and become wandering transients trying to establish their own home ranges. This is another high-risk period in a tiger's life. In fact, most transient tigers perish. Some are shot or poisoned by people when straying into marginal habitats or after killing livestock. Others get injured while hunting dangerous prey or fighting with other tigers, and starve to death.

Mortality rates are higher for transient males than for females. For one thing there are roughly three times more potential home range 'slots' available for females. Resident tigresses often make room for their daughters by yielding a portion of their ranges. Young males have to explore more aggressively, and face higher risks. They also tend to disperse farther, thus increasing the chances of passing through hostile, human-dominated landscapes. The mortality rates for transients are estimated to be as high as 30 to 35 per cent per year.

Because transient tigers can acquire home ranges only by overcoming weak resident breeders, only a few actually manage to breed. To give a crude idea of the high natural attrition rate among tigers, out of 100 cubs born, only 60 may become juveniles, 54 reach the dispersal stage and only about 20 tigers may ultimately reach the breeding age.

Once they acquire home ranges and start producing cubs, resident tigresses commonly have a tenure length of six to eight years. The competition among male breeders is more severe, and as a result, male tenures are much shorter (three to four years). Among the breeding tigers in a population, annual mortality rates are estimated at five per cent for females and 15 per cent for males.

Population Dynamics

If reliable estimates of tiger population size, age and sex ratios, fecundity and mortality rates are available, it is possible to simulate the possible working of a tiger population using computer models. Steve Kenny and his colleagues built such a model to simulate a tiger population in Chitwan. Using very different modelling methods, Brad Stith and I were able to simulate the dynamics of a tiger population with 24 breeding females. Despite the very different approaches we used, the two models produced similar results, because the birth and death rates that we plugged into both models were comparable. These models provide interesting insights into how real tiger populations may function.

Immigration of dispersing animals from outside into the population, and the emigration of dispersing animals away from it, are also factors that affect the size and dynamics of any tiger population that is connected to others. Such interlinked populations, in which sub-populations occasionally exchange individuals, are known as 'meta-populations', and their study requires more sophisticated modelling approaches.

Some conservationists suggest that it is not enough to build such purely demographic models (which predict changes in tiger numbers over time), and we have to plug in other factors, like the effects of genetic deterioration, and environmental impacts like floods or fires, to make models more realistic. It can be argued that actions of human beings, such as social instability or war, also need to be factored into tiger population models. The problem is that the effects of such complex factors on tiger birth and death rates, and population size are virtually impossible to predict.

The key factor to remember is that the more limited demographic models of tiger populations do not try to predict the future. They can only provide us with an understanding of how tiger populations may function, and what factors are likely to be more important in determining their future trajectory. For such a limited purpose, demographic models like the ones described earlier are quite useful.

Demographic models based on data from long-term tiger studies in Chitwan and Nagarahole clearly show several features that characterize a healthy tiger population: high densities of breeding females, high levels of fecundity, high rates of natural mortality, and what ecologist Paul Errington termed a 'doomed surplus': many transient tigers that are bound to perish every year. These features of wild tiger populations have an important bearing on tiger conservation, which is grossly under-appreciated by the conservation community, as we shall see later.

Population Sources and Sinks at a Landscape Level

The model of a 'working tiger population' I have described above is based on studies conducted in prime, well-protected habitats. Such productive tiger populations are, of course, not typical of most tiger habitats. Over much of the tiger's extensive distributional range, ecological conditions are very different: mortality rates are even higher for all age classes of tigers. A stage may already have been reached where even the naturally high birth rates of tigers cannot maintain population levels because few females breed to compensate for high mortalities. The annual 'doomed surplus' of transient tigers has vanished and the tiger population may be in decline.

In the temperate taiga forests of the Russian Far East, or in the tropical evergreen and mangrove forests in southern and southeast Asia, the carrying capacity of the habitat for tigers is much lower. Given the scarcity of ungulate prey, mortality rates would be higher and the proportion of 'surplus transients' low. Even in more productive deciduous forest or alluvial grassland habitats, human intrusions have dramatically lowered carrying capacities for wild tigers.

Human intrusions are many and include: hunting of ungulate prey; overgrazing by livestock that compete with wild herbivores; excessive logging and forest product collection; disruption and fragmentation of tiger landscapes due to human settlements; and roads, dams, mines and other developmental projects. In a major part of their present range, wild tiger populations have to cope with these disturbance factors.

Considering the larger fragmented landscapes as a whole, there are only a few clusters of breeding female territories within better-protected habitats or reserves that are now producing 'surpluses' of wild tigers. These protected reserves are now the only 'source' populations for tigers. The rest of Asia's forested landscapes are essentially population 'sinks' in which surplus tigers from the source populations perish. From a conservation perspective, we can readily see how vital these 'source' populations in protected areas are for the future survival of wild tigers.

A six-month-old male tiger cub.

Tigers In Retreat

Expanding Farms, Receding Forests

We know that the tiger has evolved over millennia, by hunting large ungulates through stealth and ambuscade. We also know that an average tiger needs to kill 50 such prey animals a year just to survive, and a tigress raising cubs needs as many as 70. All these biological traits of tigers place humans and their livestock right in the middle of the tiger's menu. This fact set the stage for eternal human-tiger conflict. In this chapter, we will see how conflicts between human beings and tigers manifested themselves in a fast-changing world during the last several centuries.

The human population of Asia has increased dramatically over the last few hundred years. Most Asian people are farmers or herders. Throughout history, perhaps as many as 80 to 90 per cent of Asians have lived off the land in some manner. Even now, despite increasing industrialization and the growth of mega cities, the vast majority of people in tiger range are rural folk. As a consequence of the dramatic rise of these rural populations, the need for farmland has also grown sharply. Tiger forests have been cut down extensively and replaced with crops like rice, wheat, millet, sorghum and cassava to feed more and more people.

In the era of primitive 'slash-and-burn' agriculture, forest clearance was followed by a long fallow period when the forest could grow back again. Tigers may even have benefited from such early human modifications of the landscape, particularly in tropical evergreen rainforests: the use of axe, fire and the plow created a temporary mosaic of secondary forest with an abundance of bamboo and palatable shrubs, on which the tiger's prey thrived.

However, as settled and intensive farming became the predominant form of agriculture, areas once lost by tigers to human settlement were gone forever.

Farms pushed back forests everywhere, spontaneously driven by the land hunger of an increasing rural population. However, additional social factors have aggravated such expansionist pressures. Relatively slow growth of the industrial and service sectors of the national economies has meant greater human reliance on land-based occupations and greater pressure on tiger habitats. On the political front, failure of social schemes to redistribute existing farmland more equitably among landless people resulted in further advancing of the agricultural frontier. Planned agricultural expansion projects to geographically redistribute human populations, such as the 'Transmigration' projects in Indonesia that moved thousands of people from Java to Sumatra, opened up new agricultural frontiers where none existed before.

The advancement of modern medicine, leading to the eradication of persistent endemic diseases like malaria, opened up hitherto inhospitable tiger habitats, such as those in the Himalayan foothills and the Western Ghats of India, to intensive agricultural colonization. Increasing demand for timber and commercial crops like coffee, tea, rubber, oil palm and spices attracted powerful corporations to the forestry and agriculture sector in Asia, to join the small-scale homesteaders — to be another potent force in pushing the agricultural frontier deeper and deeper into what was once the tiger's exclusive domain.

There is no doubt that cumulatively, more than any other factor, agricultural expansion has been the strongest force in

Tigers attain high densities in deciduous forests where there is abundant forage for their prey species.

shrinking the tiger habitats down to their present miniscule proportion of the Asian landscape.

Impact of Animal Husbandry

In most parts of Asia, farming and raising livestock are inseparable activities. Water buffalo, oxen and horses are used

Tiger tracks are useful indicators of their presence in an area.

for plowing the land. Livestock are raised for meat and dairy products by freely grazing on forest land. At least in southern Asia, the dung from cows and buffalos is widely used as organic manure in farms. Unlike tillage animals, these dung producers are kept in huge numbers, disproportionate to the actual cultivated area. As agriculture expanded, so have various kinds of livestock-raising activities.

Livestock like cows, buffalos, horses, donkeys, goats and pigs compete for forage with the tiger's natural prey: deer, wild cattle and wild pigs. Maintained at excessively high densities, as is the tradition in parts of Asia, these livestock can render the forests barren for wild ungulates through competition for favored forage. Wild ungulates can live at much higher densities in forests that are free of domestic livestock.

Different species of wild ungulates have co-evolved with the forests, through adaptations to feed on different plant species or different parts of plants in different seasons. Such adaptations enable several ungulate species to coexist at fairly high densities without degrading the forest. Domestic livestock are not similarly adapted, and tend to degrade the forest by overgrazing favored forage plants. In several areas of south Asia, forage has been so depleted by overgrazing that herders now have to climb trees to lop branches to feed their hungry livestock. Excessive densities of cattle compact the earth as they walk, reducing soil fertility and productivity. In the long run, such overgrazed forests are unable to support high densities of either wild ungulates or their domesticated cousins, thereby lowering the carrying capacity for tigers.

Sometimes wild ungulates are infected by diseases transmitted by domestic stock. For instance, during the 1960s, hundreds of gaur died in the forests of southern India from an outbreak of rinderpest spread by cattle that grazed freely in the forests.

Whenever livestock enter their habitats, tigers readily kill them. Even if wild prey is present, it is often easier for tigers to kill domestic stock whose anti-predator responses tend to be poorer. When wild prey is scarce, tigers persistently hunt livestock. Such predation inevitably leads to conflict with the herders, and, as inevitably, to the retaliatory killing of tigers.

Exploitation of Forest Products

The forests that harbor tigers also contain many other products of utility or commercial value to humans. As the overall forest resource base of the planet has shrunk from past over-exploitation, the value of remaining forest products has skyrocketed.

*Protected nature reserves offer the best prospect for the long-term survival of wild
tiger populations. Reserves that harbor tigers also protect many other forms of biodiversity.*

The penetration of roads into remote tiger habitats attracts market-linked hunting and forest exploitation into such areas.

Timber trees are the most obvious example of such a commercial resource: the oaks and pines in the temperate forests, dipterocarps of the tropical rainforests and teak in the deciduous forests, produce timber for the construction industry and furniture making. The timbers used in decorative laminates and perfumeries are even more valuable. Therefore, timber harvesting, both by the organized industrial sector and by the unorganized rural sector – legally as well as illegally – exerts a major pressure on tiger habitats almost everywhere.

In southern, western and central Asia, removal of wood-fuel for cooking and pole crop of younger trees for house building is an even greater threat to forests than cutting larger timber. In many parts of India and Nepal, unsustainable collection of fuel wood by villagers is laying waste huge tracts of forests. Unfortunately, in response to the soaring demand for fuel wood in urban markets, its collection and sale have emerged as a profitable occupation for many rural people.

The case is similar with the exploitation of bamboo, rattan and thatch grass in many forests, particularly in south Asia. Some of these plants provide forage to the tiger's prey and shelter to the tigers too. Their removal has an even more direct negative impact on tigers, often more severe than the removal of valuable timber. Many products in the tiger's habitats are eagerly coveted by an expanding human population. While listing them exhaustively is beyond the scope of this book, the following examples will give an idea of the range of non-timber forest products exploited commercially: ginseng and other roots, leaves, flowers, fruits, nuts, resins and even the bark of many tree species. These products flow out of the forest to meet the needs of growing industrial markets for branded products in the pharmaceutical, processed-food, perfume and chemical industries.

Such removals of forest products may not always show an immediate adverse affect on tigers or their principal prey, as they would, say, on monkeys or fruit-eating birds. However, the complex, naturally evolved linkages between plant and animal elements in the forest are still unexplored. Therefore, what long-term consequences the forest product exploitation will have on forest structure and animals, is virtually unknown at present.

What is known is that forest product exploitation invariably means intrusion of roads and people into tiger habitats. These people often sustain themselves by hunting wild ungulates. Sometimes they hunt tigers too. Very often they settle down with their livestock and start agriculture, expanding the farming frontier. Thus, almost inevitably, forest exploitation projects result in new roads, transportation methods, equipment and the human settlements taking root in wilderness areas. But their most devastating consequence is the penetration of forces of global commerce in forest and wildlife products into the tiger's domain. Such commerce can overnight turn a humble local villager collecting wild honey in a remote forest of India into a poacher who supplies tiger bones to a trader in Hong Kong.

Impact of Forest Fires

Arson is a conservation problem peculiar to tiger habitats in some dry forests of Asia. Local people deliberately burn forests for a variety of reasons: to promote growth of grass for their cattle; to facilitate the search for and collection of non-timber forest products; to clear undergrowth for safety from wild elephants. Some fires are lit accidentally, while others are a form of protest against authority. While a patchy forest burn once in several years probably does not damage tiger habitats, regular, deliberate arson has caused serious degradation in many areas. V. G. Heptner has recorded how deliberate arson virtually eliminated tiger habitats in parts of western and central Asia, even a century ago.

Developmental Projects

Until about 50 years ago, all the 13 countries that now harbor wild tigers were under colonial or feudal rulers. There was no impetus for rapid industrial growth and economic development. Things changed rapidly when national liberation movements and the democratization of society picked up pace. During the

Steel traps made tiger killing safe and easy for poachers.

last 50 years, as these countries have become self-governing, all of them have set rapid economic development as a central social goal. Projects for developing national agriculture, or economy, or for addressing pressing social problems, have burgeoned as a result.

Networks of roads, railways and waterways have intruded into formerly inaccessible tiger habitats in remote regions. Giant projects for mining, irrigation and power generation have erupted like rashes over relatively intact tiger landscapes. River valley and mining projects in particular have torn out large chunks of productive tiger habitats.

Developmental projects are harbingers of specific problems for tigers. Large reservoirs may inundate critical habitats.

Opencast mines cause severe soil erosion and siltation in rivers downstream from them. Industrial plants may discharge toxic chemicals into their surroundings. All these impacts have serious long-term consequences for the health and stability of the ecosystems of which tiger habitats are a part.

Although the area lost to such developmental projects is relatively small in comparison to the area of tiger habitats lost by conversion to cropland, in absolute terms it is substantial. However, a far more serious consequence of such developmental projects has been the fragmentation and disruption of tiger habitats. Although tigers can move through almost any kind of cover, large breaks in forest continuity caused by densely populated human settlements sever the connectivity between tiger populations.

Development projects, particularly roads, allow the influx of immigrants and new technologies into remote tiger habitats. Roads and railways also allow rapid transportation of forest and wildlife products outwards. In general, opening up a remote, hitherto inaccessible area because of a new development project usually has all the broadly negative consequences of advancing the human settlements into tiger habitats already discussed.

Hunting and Poaching of Tigers

People have hunted tigers for a variety of reasons: most commonly to protect livestock, and less often for protecting human lives. Much of the bounty hunting of tigers in the past two centuries was for the above reasons. Tigers also have been hunted for 'sport' in all cultures, to collect their skin, teeth or claws as trophies, and for commercial reasons to supply the large and profitable market for their body parts created by the practice of traditional medicine in oriental cultures.

Aboriginal and rural people in Asia have hunted tigers for hundreds of years. They used native fieldcraft and knowledge of

*During the early 1990s evidence emerged of heavy poaching pressure on tigers to meet the demand for their bones.
Tigers in the Russian Far East became vulnerable to such pressures. Special anti-poaching squads, established with financial
support from international donors, were helpful in countering this threat from organized tiger poaching.*

the tiger's habits with great ingenuity, to devise methods for killing tigers, well before the advent of the gun. Cooperative hunting is one such technique. For example, the Uppaliga, a rural community in the south Indian state of Karnataka, have a brave tradition of driving tigers into nets and spearing them at close quarters.

Several kinds of pit traps, in which sharp stakes are buried, are deployed to kill tigers. Attracted by a baited prey, the tiger walks across the cleverly concealed pit, falls in, and impales itself. The Bagmari, a professional tribe of tiger hunters in north India, deploy booby traps with bows and arrows to kill tigers attracted to animal carcasses. Korean and Russian hunters rode horseback and killed tigers by spearing or archery. Often dogs are used to track and corner tigers, while the hunters move in for the kill.

Many tribal people in Asia have traditionally employed snares and deadfall traps to catch large ungulates. Although not meant to catch tigers, occasionally tigers do die in these devices. Tigers were often caught in wooden traps using live baits and then killed. In the grassland habitats at the foothills of the Himalayas an easy method of getting rid of tigers is to burn down the patch of grass in which tiger cubs are sheltering.

It is important to realize that a wild tiger has only got to be injured seriously, not necessarily killed outright, as a result of being hunted. Gangrene, infections and starvation are often the ultimate agents that kill a tiger that escapes from hunters.

There is no doubt that thousands of tigers perished in such native contraptions before the Asian hunters learnt to use steel and gunpowder imported from the west. There is also no doubt that many brave men perished while hunting tigers using the archaic techniques described above. Tiger hunting was clearly recognized as a dangerous activity, and a man who vanquished a tiger was considered a hero in almost all Asian cultures. However, despite widespread persecution, the tiger's adaptability and high fecundity ensured its survival.

With the arrival of rolled or drawn steel in the form of plates, cables and spring wire, things began to change rapidly for tigers. Steel in these more malleable forms became widely available. Snares and jaw-traps that were strong enough to hold tigers were made from steel components, and could be hidden on paths that the tigers regularly used. Once caught, a tiger is rendered practically immobile and could be easily speared or shot to death. The professional hunter's job became easy: he had merely to set his traps at good spots and wait at home until a tiger was caught.

However, it was the arrival of guns that decisively tilted the balance against the tiger in this war of attrition. Until then only the very brave or the very crafty among the natives could hunt tigers. With a gun in hand, almost anybody could kill a tiger… and did. Tiger shooting became a popular pastime among kings and commoners, both native and colonial. In combination with shooting, older methods of cornering wild tigers, such as the pit traps, jaw traps, beats, netting, hunting dogs and booby traps, all became even more effective. Once a tiger was trapped or cornered in some manner, shooting it was a relatively simple matter.

Guns also made it possible to use other traditions, such as riding elephants, to hunt tigers. The beat method of hunting tigers, which deployed riding elephants, became popular with the royalty who could afford it. Waiting for tigers at live baits or kills became a highly effective and safe method to shoot tigers.

As a result, hunters of all sorts slaughtered tigers on a massive scale during the nineteenth and twentieth centuries. Particularly bloodthirsty hunters came from the privileged social classes, as the following few examples show: Gordon-Cummings shot 73 tigers during 1863-64 in a single district in central India; King George V and his entourage shot 39 tigers in Nepal in 11 days in 1911-12, while the King of Nepal and guests shot 433 tigers between 1933-40. Colonel Nightingale shot over 300 tigers in southern India, while the Maharajas of Udaipur and of Surguja both killed over 1000 tigers in their provinces. Although such individual tallies of tigers killed sound horrific today, numerous local poachers and bounty hunters killed perhaps as many tigers as these 'sportsmen' did. Historian Mahesh Rangarajan estimates that in a few parts of India more than 80,000 tigers were killed either for 'sport' or bounties between 1875 and 1925.

Following World War II, an array of new inventions arrived on the tiger's doorstep. In addition to the vastly improved quality of guns and ammunition, a most effective hunting aid was the portable flashlight powered by dry-cell batteries. Flashlights allowed night hunting, enabling shooters to 'freeze' their quarry in a beam and kill it safely from a tree hide or vehicle. The easy availability of cheap, war-surplus Jeeps provided hunters greater access and mobility in tiger habitats.

In the post-war period, chemical insecticides such as DDT, used to eradicate malarial mosquitoes, and the chlorinated hydrocarbons developed to protect crops from insects, became freely available. In the hands of millions of farmers engaged in pushing back the forest frontier, these pesticides became the most efficient means of exterminating tigers all over their range. Carcasses of livestock killed by tigers were poisoned with pesticides, killing whole families of tigers. Occasionally, instead of chemical poisons, home-made bombs of dynamite and steel shrapnel were buried in livestock carcasses, blowing away the jaws of any unlucky tiger that fed on the kill.

Another technique recently used in India to poach tigers is electrocution. High-voltage electricity, illegally tapped from the power mains, is used to energize hidden trip wires laid across the paths of passing animals. Tigers and other animals that use these paths are easily killed with this method.

Trade in Tiger Body Parts

In whatever manner tigers are killed, their body parts are considered to be of great value for a variety of cultural reasons. Tiger skins, claws, and teeth have been valued as trophies and talismans for centuries all over the world. Eating tiger meat is considered healthy even in India, where people worship the animal as a deity.

However, a major threat to wild tigers is from the consumption of their body parts as an integral part of the traditional system of medicine practiced in oriental cultures of China, Taiwan, Japan, Tibet, Singapore and Korea. From centuries of tradition, roughly a quarter of humanity truly believes that consuming tiger bones can cure arthritis and strengthen muscles, tiger blood is a tonic, tiger tail can cure skin disease and eating the cat's eyeballs can get rid of cataracts.

China alone has a billion humans who regard traditional Chinese medicine (TCM) as a legitimate healthcare system. It is also a country of enterprising natives, which shares a border with seven other tiger range countries. Expatriate Chinese in other countries also exercise consumer pressure for tiger products. These TCM consumers are a large, growing and profitable market for the illegal tiger trade. Highly organized networks of wildlife traders scour forested regions of Asia, looking for poachers who can supply them with tiger parts. Such suppliers may be organized poaching gangs that deliberately hunt tigers or simply local villagers who sometimes opportunistically shoot or poison tigers in their neighborhoods.

After international tiger conservation efforts were launched in the early 1970s, the Convention on International Trade in Endangered Species (CITES) based in Geneva, to which most nations are signatories, gradually tightened up the rules against international (but not domestic) trade in tiger parts, culminating in a total international trade ban in 1987. However, in the early 1990s national authorities and non-governmental organizations monitoring wildlife trade, such as TRAFFIC, noted a surge in seizures of illegally killed wild tigers in India, Russia and parts of Asia. Tiger poaching appeared to have increased, as park protection declined because of social factors.

For example, following a sting operation in 1993, a single seizure in India yielded 1100 lb (500 kg) of tiger bones. It was

Tigers cannot survive where their prey base has been depleted.

clear that the bulk of the supplies, originating from tiger habitats in India, Russia and other countries, were being traded illegally. An analysis of incomplete trade records by Judy Mills and her colleagues in TRAFFIC showed that, between 1970 and 1993, bones from about 500 to 1000 tigers were traded legally. These dead tigers had apparently come from Hong Kong, Thailand, Indonesia and China before the trade ban was applied.

Prey Depletion

So far we have looked at factors that caused a dramatic shrinkage in the tiger's original range, and continue to reduce the extent of its habitat. We have seen how pressures from

farming, livestock raising, forest product collection and large developmental projects break up and degrade the physical quality of the habitats in which the tigers have to survive. Yet despite these pressures, a substantial amount of habitat that is potentially suitable for tigers still exists in Asia. According to an assessment made by the Wildlife Conservation Society and World Wildlife Fund-U.S.A. in 1997, about 580,000 sq miles (1.5 million sq km) of habitat potentially suitable for tigers still survives in the world. However, populations of wild tigers that breed well, and produce a surplus for dispersal, occupy only a tiny fraction of the potential habitat available. There is still a lot of habitat, but there are no tigers in it.

Why are most Asian forests empty of tigers? The single most important reason appears to be the destruction of the tiger's prey base, rather than direct killing of tigers. The vast majority of rural and forest people in Asia (with the exception of some priestly and mercantile castes in India) are meat eaters, although many of them practice Hindu and Buddhist religions that, in principle, oppose the killing of animals. Most of them are not subsistence hunters in the sense that Inuit people of the Arctic or the Pygmies in central Africa are. Crops and livestock provide their primary source of food. However, some Asians hunt wildlife for entertainment and for luxury consumption.

Most Asian hunters are not professionals who focus on tiger hunting, nor are they rich sport-hunters interested in tiger trophies; they are primarily rural folk who hunt wild ungulates, monkeys, game birds and large reptiles. They eat the animals they kill, often sharing them with their kin. They may sell part of a kill to petty traders in wildlife products for cash, which helps them to buy ammunition to go hunting again. Although these hunters don't make huge profits or derive most of their nutrition from wild animals, hunting is very much a part of their social life. The proportion of such hunters could be quite small in the rural populace, as in parts of south Asia, or it could be fairly high, as it is in southeast Asia and Russia.

Asian hunters kill wild ungulates using a diverse array of techniques that often combine native fieldcraft and ethno-biology with modern tools and weapons. Wild ungulates are commonly killed by shooting, snaring or trapping.

Commonly, snares made of plant fibers — and recently of steel cables — are placed across ungulate trails. In remote areas of Laos, biologists report that whole hillsides are strewn with wire snares, sometimes with rotting carcasses of animals that the hunters did not even return to collect. Bows capable of firing poisoned or plain arrows, stones, or even clay shots, are sometimes used, with deadly accuracy, as are pit-fall and dead-fall traps. However, with increasing availability of guns, shooting with the aid of spotlights, dogs and from vehicles has become a common mode of hunting. The guns used are often cheap, and made locally by village artisans.

Asian hunters come from all social classes. Commonly they are poor or landless people. However, often they are the village or small town élite — landowners and rich farmers — who have the money, leisure and social power to indulge in hunting. Although hunters of the tiger's ungulate prey do not form a majority of the rural Asian population, in absolute terms they add up to a huge number… several million people at least. Because of their sheer numbers, hunters have a massive impact on populations of ungulate prey, and consequently on tiger populations.

In the previous chapter, we saw how tiger population density, survival rates and chance of persistence are all strongly tied to the densities of principal prey. Through a massive overkill of their prey base, hunters have depressed carrying capacities and even eliminated tigers over most of Asia. A simple rule of thumb can assess this deadly impact: for every 50 deer hunted in a year, there is room for one less tiger on this earth.

Cumulative Impact of Humans on Tigers

Wild tigers have absorbed the impact of all the pressures enumerated above, not one after another sequentially, but at the same time. Their impacts are synergistic: the consequences of habitat loss, tiger hunting and prey depletion reinforce each other, and thus have a cumulative impact that is far greater than the sum of each individual factor.

For example, over-hunting of prey increases the female range size, reduces the number of cubs born and increases the daily and annual foraging range and movements of tigers. The impact of the direct killing of an individual tiger on the population is far greater under these circumstances than when the tiger population is at a higher density and producing surpluses. Increased foraging range is likely to bring tigers into greater contact with human settlements, increasing chances of livestock killing, and the consequent retaliation.

Opening new agricultural frontiers increases the likelihood of tigers coming into adversarial contact with humans. Developmental projects and roads increase the penetration of the agricultural frontier and commercial markets into remote regions. Such increased access, in turn, triggers spiralling commercial demands for forest products and efforts to meet these.

Given the magnitude of these synergistic forces it is almost a miracle that wild tigers have survived at least in a part of their former range. Doubtless, their remarkable ecological resilience has been a major factor underlying the persistence of tiger populations.

However, we must not forget that we humans too have also played a critical role in the survival of tigers, particularly through the last century. How we have strived to save the tiger — an enemy we also admire — makes a compelling story.

The charismatic tiger has been central to conservation efforts in Asia.

The Enemy We Admire

Tiger Conservation Initiatives: 1900-1960

During the nineteenth century, many colonial powers seized large chunks of tiger forests in Asia to protect timber reserves from encroaching agriculture. Later, in the first half of the twentieth century, in response to apprehensions of élite sport-hunters about the rapid destruction of game by 'native poachers', attempts were made in some tiger range nations under colonial rule, to set up game reserves. Usually these reserves were established exclusively for the ruling élite to hunt big game. Game reserves were also established in the post-revolution Soviet Union.

At the end of World War II new social pressures were unleashed. In tiger range nations like India, Myanmar, China, Indonesia and Malaysia, the political power to make decisions that affected conservation passed from British, French and Dutch colonial administrators into the hands of native political leaders. The colonial administrators were men from the upper classes, who were interested in perpetuating their favored sport of tiger hunting. The British, in particular, had a deep interest in natural history. The Asian leaders who replaced them usually came from different social backgrounds, and did not have much of an interest in natural history. They had more pressing priorities before them: industrialization, economic development, increasing food production and raising the living standards of their people. These new leaders commonly viewed forests as a source of logging revenue and as a frontier to be pushed back to make room for agriculture. Tigers were considered as pests to be got rid of. Although such attitudes prevailed in all the countries with wild tigers, they were most strongly manifested in China, where all-out efforts were made to eradicate tigers in the 1950s.

During the quarter century after the war, western and local 'sportsmen' were the sole advocates of the cause of tiger conservation in Asia. Only a handful of Asian naturalists, like Salim Ali in India and Boonsong Lekagul in Thailand, pleaded the cause of wildlife conservation with the political leaders of their countries. Persistent efforts by some sport hunters led to the passing of some early legislation to curb illegal hunters. However, for the most part, these anti-poaching laws were weak and poorly enforced. Most countries did not have separate departments that enforced wildlife protection laws. They entrusted this task to the forestry departments, which were usually too preoccupied with timber production to worry about tigers.

In theory at least, licensed hunters were expected to be the guardians of the forest blocks in which they had monopoly rights to hunt tigers. Such arrangements were moderately successful during the colonial era. Licensed hunters – usually colonial officials or local rulers – had some capacity to deter the native poachers by being present in the shooting blocks. This power of deterrence waned with the advent of democracy in the post-colonial period. As a result, both legal and illegal hunters worked side-by-side, seriously depleting tiger and prey populations, until the 1960s.

In the 1960s a new kind of hunter arrived on the Asian tiger scene. Following the African model, companies that catered to wealthy foreign clients who wanted to shoot tigers mushroomed, particularly in India and Nepal: these were by then the only countries where tigers could be found in reasonable numbers. Such organized safari hunting, super-imposed on existing pressure from local hunters and poachers,

Even small populations of tigers can be recovered through effective protection.

almost drove the tiger to the brink of extinction within a decade.

Recent Conservation Initiatives: 1960-1990

Many of the global tiger conservation initiatives launched after the 1960s had some connection or other with India, a country that harbored more wild tigers than any other. Publication of Richard Perry's *World of the Tiger* and George Schaller's *Deer and the Tiger* brought the precarious plight of wild tigers to the attention of the world. Questionnaire surveys on the status of Indian tigers carried out by J.C. Daniel of Bombay Natural History Society and an official assessment by Kailash Sankhala, both indicated that wild tigers were in serious trouble in India.

The general assembly of the World Conservation Union (IUCN) met in the Indian capital of New Delhi in 1969. This is considered by many to be the watershed event that energized global tiger conservation. Effective backroom lobbying by Guy Mountfort, Peter Jackson and other conservationists associated with IUCN and the World Wildlife Fund, brought the tiger crisis to the attention of a global audience. The then Indian Prime Minister, Indira Gandhi, took the lead in providing political leadership to tiger conservation. The IUCN assembly passed a resolution urging all tiger range countries to ban tiger hunting and called for the establishment of effectively protected tiger reserves. The tiger was classified as an endangered species.

Following the IUCN resolution, many tiger range countries introduced official bans on tiger hunting. Several countries, led by India, passed tough new laws that accorded protected status to tigers, prey species and some of their critical habitats. Some other countries, torn by wars and other more pressing problems, either passed relatively weak laws or did not move forward on the issue.

However, passing laws to protect tigers was one thing, implementing them effectively on the ground was another thing. In most tiger range countries efforts to actually implement the new tiger protection laws were rather hesitant and weak. There were several reasons for this lack of progress.

Many countries lacked a social ethos that would tolerate the very idea of protecting 'dangerous' animals like tigers. Hunting wildlife in general, and tigers in particular, was considered a brave and worthy pursuit. Hunting of prey species was a widespread tradition and seen as essential for protecting crops. The oriental countries in particular had a long-held tradition of using tiger body parts in their indigenous medicinal systems. Trade in tiger body parts earned substantial profits. Often such hunting meant some extra food or cash. So unless strong physical force was applied to the task of stopping hunting – through armed patrols and other anti-hunting measures – people were not going to give up hunting tigers and prey species merely because of the new laws.

Most governments in tiger range countries did not have trained park protection forces or wildlife services capable of effectively enforcing the new laws. Although some countries had forestry departments, these often lacked law enforcement powers and skills. The broader level of social support necessary to initiate effective tiger protection was absent in most countries. Such a force would not come into being merely because foreign agencies like IUCN recommended that it be so. There had to be strong pressure groups within the tiger range countries. Because most range nations lacked such pressure groups, the demand for enforcement of the new laws was muted.

Then there was the question of political support. As we have seen, tiger conservation areas can be sustained only by restricting their over-exploitation by people. Hunting, forest product collection, livestock grazing and developmental projects would inevitably have to be curtailed to make more room for wild tigers. These were politically unpopular measures, and political leaders were not usually enthusiastic about such practical necessities of tiger conservation. Therefore, in most

range nations the political leaders did not treat tiger conservation as a priority item on their agendas.

Lacking a forceful local advocacy of the tiger's cause, bereft of political support and enforcement authorities, the new tiger conservation laws remained merely as entries on the pages of statute books in most Asian countries.

However, the situation in India and Nepal was somewhat exceptional. There was strong political support for conservation because of Indira Gandhi's deep personal interest in natural history in India, and King Birendra's keen interest in sport hunting in Nepal. Both these leaders provided a decisive push to on-the-ground implementation of tiger conservation laws. India had a century-old forestry service that possessed substantial manpower and law enforcement capacity. The Nepalese government harnessed its fierce Gurkha army for the task.

In India, a vocal lobby of middle-class conservationists effectively advocated the tiger's cause through the free press. In Nepal, a strong American interest in wildlife nurtured by the Smithsonian Institution and the local tourism industry played a similar advocacy role. As a result, both these south Asian nations quickly and effectively established several fine protected areas for tigers. Some of the best tiger habitats in the world today – Kanha, Bandipur, Nagarahole, Ranthambore and Chitwan among others – were all recovered from the brink of disaster in the early 1970s.

An underlying social factor helped the establishment of tiger reserves in India and Nepal. In both countries the predominant Hindu religion accepted the basic idea that in addition to humans, other species too have a right to survive on this planet. While this broad philosophy did not stop people from killing tigers or their prey, it certainly helped them to accept the establishment of protected areas in their localities with a greater degree of tolerance than almost anywhere else in the world. The Hindu sense of guilt at killing an animal (even the most

inveterate meat-eaters turn vegetarian when ritual demands) made it easier for the reserve staff to prosecute poachers.

Another unique feature of the tiger conservation efforts in India deserves a brief mention. Although international financial assistance helped to improve tiger protection measures, contrary to the general impression it formed less than a tenth

Tigers are major tourist attractions in India and Nepal.

of the total investment made by India in tiger conservation efforts. Furthermore, if the amount of logging revenues that were forgone were included, local investments in tiger conservation would increase by many times more.

There is no doubt that tiger population recovery efforts came not a moment too soon for south Asia. Nowhere else in the entire tiger range, except perhaps in China, was the tiger habitat as reduced and fragmented. The human population density was very high and pressures on tiger habitats intense.

In other parts of tiger range countries, where human population density and related pressures are comparable to India and Nepal – such as in the productive lowland areas of Indonesia, Thailand and south China – tigers were extirpated during the same period. However, relatively large areas of tropical rainforests survived in hilly regions of these countries. Sumatra in Indonesia, peninsular Malaysia, Myanmar, Thailand, Cambodia, Laos and Vietnam harbored large blocks of tropical

Breeding wild tigers in India are mainly found in protected areas.

rainforests in the 1970s. Their sheer size, and remoteness from the advancing agricultural frontier, provided sanctuary for tigers. Consequently, even in the absence of effective anti-hunting measures, tigers and their prey managed to survive at low densities in these rainforests.

Furthermore, two social factors appear to have favored the

survival of tigers in Sumatra and Peninsular Malaysia. A substantial proportion of the population in these regions practice Islam, whose followers do not eat pork. Therefore, wild pigs and tapirs are not widely hunted for their meat, and provide a stable prey base for tigers, despite the depletion of other principal prey such as sambar, banteng and gaur.

Secondly, extensive primary rainforests that are poor habitats for tigers have turned into secondary forests due to logging impacts. Some secondary forests can provide more forage for large ungulates, and can thus support higher densities of tigers. Recent camera-trap surveys in Malaysia suggest that tigers indeed attain higher densities in such secondary forests, compared to primary rainforests. However, wherever logged primary forest areas are planted with oil palm or other crops, the tiger habitat is lost forever.

The tiger conservation initiatives of the 1960s were too little and too late for many tigers of the world. The tigers in the Caspian region and in the Indonesian island of Java blinked out in the 1970s. Tigers in most parts of southeast Asia declined. Tigers of southern China, victims of a local culture that valued the big cat only for its body parts, were driven into virtual extinction. The northernmost wild tigers fared much better and survived in Russia, and on the Chinese side of the international border.

Through the 1970s and 1980s tiger populations recovered in sporadic patches in southern Asia and in Russia, and made isolated gains in a few reserves in Thailand, Indonesia and Malaysia. Wherever tiger populations recovered, it was always in response to strong preservationist policies that squarely met the tiger's ecological needs by reducing adverse human impacts. The deployment of armed patrols was crucial in reducing the illegal hunting of tigers and their prey. Eliminating logging and non-timber forest product collection was another major step. In south Asia, regulation of livestock grazing and fuel wood collection also played a critical role. Erection of barriers separating tiger habitats from human settlements, control over man-made forest fires, and creation of additional water resources, were also important factors in improving the habitat quality for prey species and tigers within protected areas. However, outside a few of these areas, tigers continued to decline in numbers in all the range countries: the overall tiger range shrank as populations splintered into ever smaller fragments.

Despite this grim background, a sense of optimism was evident among conservationists by the early 1980s. This optimism was based largely on increasing tiger numbers that the Asian managers were reporting. However, the methods they used to generate most of these tiger numbers were unscientific: consequently, the tiger numbers were mostly unreliable. They showed that tigers were increasing at biologically unrealistic rates over large regions, states and even countries. This proposition was clearly at odds with reality. Despite this, international conservation agencies widely circulated the 'tiger numbers' generated by Asian managers, lending them credibility in the eyes of the public.

At the International Parks Congress held in Bali in 1982, a manager from India even posed a rhetorical question: what do you do after you have succeeded in saving tigers? International conservation agencies, eager for success stories, were beginning to believe that tiger conservation efforts were succeeding. The fact that the spectacular tiger population recovery was sporadic and restricted to a few tiger reserves in southern Asia was simply lost sight of.

Shifting Paradigms Affect Conservation: 1980-1990

Even as overoptimistic views about the tiger's prospects were being aired, major paradigm shifts were taking place in the international conservation arena. These shifts radically affected the way in which the tiger conservation agenda was pursued later.

As we saw earlier, human activities such as hunting, agriculture, livestock raising, forest product collection and developmental projects have negative impacts on tigers. However, regulating such activities in tiger habitats causes inconvenience to the people living next to tigers. Quite naturally, rural people resented these impositions, which they saw as a price only they were forced to pay for saving tigers. Very often social mechanisms to address people's grievances were inadequate or non-existent. This does not mean that the preservationist measures were unnecessary, but that in many cases the affected local people were not compensated adequately.

In the 1980s ideas called 'sustainable use' and 'sustainable development' entered the conservation lexicon. These propositions argued that wildlife and biodiversity could be saved not by establishing protected areas that kept out human impacts, but by encouraging human uses in a manner compatible with conservation goals. While 'sustainable use' sounded like an attractive alternative to protected reserves – and indeed it was for some forms of biodiversity – it was undoubtedly a harmful prescription for ecologically vulnerable species like tigers. Habitats that supported breeding tiger populations had already shrunk to about one per cent of their former range, as a result of human use. More of the same could only make things worse for tigers.

The real problem with sustainable use was in the ecological mismatch between numbers of consumers as opposed to the size of the biological resource base. By 1980s the market economy had penetrated the remotest parts of the tigers' range, and enormously increased the material aspirations of people everywhere. New technologies, combined with traditional skills, permitted even more severe exploitation of forest and wildlife products. There was no basis for the belief that the linkages between rising human numbers, increasing aspirations and growing global markets could be the basis for

sustainable use of tiger habitats, if such 'sustainability' meant the viability and integrity of tiger habitats and populations. Yet, integrated conservation and development projects (ICDP) with 'sustainable use' as their keystone became the dominant trend in international conservation.

The international aid agencies that promoted 'sustainable use' played a central role in shaping the economies and developmental policies of most debt-ridden tiger range countries. The latter were suffering from political instability and economic upheavals (modernization in China, the break-up of the Soviet Union, political instability in India, Indonesia and Indochina, for example). Consequent austerity measures cut funding for core resources needed for tiger protection, such as staff, vehicles and infrastructure.

At the same time, international agencies subtly, but firmly, demanded a shift away from the earlier preservation-oriented approach, towards new policies that encouraged park managers to implement development activities outside tiger reserves, to enlist local support. These new policy prescriptions were backed up by massive loans. Managers of tiger reserves, who had been engaged in the hard, thankless task of protection, readily took to the diversions offered by these new ideas. As a result of this paradigm shift, tiger protection efforts were seriously undercut during the 1990s.

Dealing With a New Tiger Crisis: 1990-1997

In the 1990s evidence emerged that the illegal trade in tiger body parts was much larger than earlier estimated. Monitoring of trade statistics by international agencies revealed increasing volumes of consumption and trade in tiger body parts in China, Taiwan, Korea, Japan and among the expatriate oriental communities in many parts of the world.

In 1993-94, undercover sting operations in India led to seizures of massive stocks of illegally hoarded tiger body parts.

In a single seizure, local authorities assisted by TRAFFIC's informers seized bones estimated to have come from about 60 tigers. Subsequent undercover work by conservationists and police led to many large hauls of tiger products in India, Nepal, and Russia. Under interrogation, the arrested poachers confessed that declining park protection had allowed them to operate freely even within protected tiger reserves.

A new tiger crisis appeared to have struck. The suddenness and scale of these discoveries shattered the complacency of tiger conservationists and local governments about their having 'succeeded in saving the tiger'. Their reactions, as with their earlier claims of success, were in the form of somewhat overblown rhetoric.

Peter Jackson, Chairman of the IUCN Cat Specialist group and an early advocate of tiger preservation, made the dire prediction that wild tigers would be virtually extinct by the end of the twentieth century. This somewhat simplistic message of superstitious orientals eating their way through the world's supply of tigers was widely embraced. Catchy sound bites about the bone trade driving wild tigers into extinction by the turn of the century were picked up and amplified by the media. These echo, even to this day, in most media reports of tiger conservation issues.

The strong reaction to the 'new tiger crisis' did some good, at least in the short run. Following worldwide concern and concerted action by IUCN, CITES, TRAFFIC, WWF, WCS and other conservation agencies, the United States Government threatened to impose potentially damaging trade sanctions against countries that had lax laws and enforcement protocols against illegal tiger trade. China, South Korea and Taiwan responded swiftly to the threat of sanctions, and tightened up their enforcement efforts. Major public education campaigns were launched in China, Hong Kong and Singapore to educate TCM consumers about the terrible impact they were having on the wild tigers of the world. As a result, at least the brazen, open sale of tiger products became scarce after 1995, and although the illegal tiger trade did not stop, its volume probably declined. However, the clandestine nature of the trade makes it very difficult to assess its volume or impact.

Some practitioners of traditional Chinese medicine and believers in free-market economics argue that legal farming and slaughter of tigers is the only practical solution to the problem of regulating the illegal tiger trade. However, most tiger conservationists and trade regulators believe that such a remedy may be worse than the disease. They argue that: re-establishment of a legal market for tigers will again increase poaching pressure on wild tigers; it will permit the 'laundering' of illegally killed wild tigers as 'farmed tigers' and generally counter the efforts to educate the public about the ecological and esthetic value of wild tigers. Animal rights activists highlight the cruelty involved in tiger farming and slaughter, pointing out the horrendous conditions under which tigers are currently being 'farmed' under the guise of 'captive breeding'.

Another solution being tried out examines the possibility of using substitute products derived from domesticated or abundant animals to satisfy the traditional Chinese medicine consumers. However, before it can work, practitioners who prescribe tiger remedies have to be convinced that the alternatives offered are indeed effective. Because most of them do not accept the models of scientific research used elsewhere, it is not easy to 'prove' the efficacy of substitute products. However, since 1995 tiger conservationists, trade regulators and doctors who practice traditional medicine have met face-to-face, engendering mutual trust and understanding, in an effort to resolve this vexed problem.

Reversing the Tiger's Decline

Although initially useful, the predictions of the tiger's imminent extinction, and the attribution of the trade in tiger parts as the single most important factor driving it, have also caused some setbacks to tiger conservation by diverting attention away from critical issues.

Firstly, the predictions have bred a deep despondency and pessimism about the prospects for wild tigers in the general public, particularly in developed countries. Many conservationists based in western zoos subtly argued that the situation in tiger range countries was so grim that western zoos were like modern 'arks' which would ultimately be the only places where tigers could survive in the near future. Therefore, they urged huge investments in captive-breeding and assisted reproduction facilities, so that tigers could be reintroduced into their native homes, if and when tiger range countries managed to establish truly protected areas. Thus, the pessimism about wild tigers diverted substantial funding towards captive breeding as a major plank for conserving tigers.

More importantly, highlighting trade-driven poaching as the single most important cause of tiger decline obscured the real long-term threat to tiger conservation: declining commitment to protected areas for tigers that are free from incompatible human activities. Measures for tackling the tiger trade problem, such as catching traders, tightening trade laws or educating consumers of tiger products, simply did not deal with the core issue of preserving the tiger's prey base and habitat in the wild.

Thirdly, in the absence of reliable data on tiger numbers and trade-related hunting, it is difficult to judge the real impact of the illegal tiger trade on tiger numbers. As we saw earlier, in each productive tiger population there is an annual surplus of animals that is dispersing into and perishing in the surrounding landscape. If poaching is simply removing a part of this surplus, it may not have a major influence in determining tiger population trajectories. Also, it is not clear if the tiger poaching detected in the early 1990s was an emerging new threat, or was something

In prey-rich habitats, tigresses can produce more cubs than the area can support.
Such productive wild tiger populations can take some degree of poaching pressure without going into a decline.

that had been going on for years without being detected.

The lack of reliable information has been a major problem in making rational decisions and prioritizing conservation actions to save wild tigers. In 1997 the Zoological Society of London, in association with the Save the Tiger Fund, sponsored by the National Fish and Wildlife Foundation and the Exxon Corporation, organized a meeting of the world's leading tiger scientists and conservationists in London's Regent's Park Zoo. The aim was to try to synthesize the information from ongoing studies. Several major studies converged on two central issues.

Firstly, it became clear that the loss of prey base due to local over-hunting was a critically important factor in driving the decline of wild tigers. Field studies in India, Russia, Indochina and Sumatra, as well as computer modelling work, showed that prey depletion was likely to be a more important causal factor in the tiger's decline than trade-related poaching.

Secondly, almost all the ongoing tiger studies highlighted the need for having protected areas that were patrolled effectively to keep out illegal hunters and other pressures on habitats. While community-based conservation and eco-tourism appear to hold promise for gaining greater public support on the edges of reserves, the keystone of tiger conservation still has to be a network of strictly protected nature reserves. The decline in commitment to such effectively protected areas, even in India, which had a strong record earlier, appeared to be a critical factor driving the tiger crisis.

The drift away from core issues of tiger conservation had occurred in a knowledge vacuum. The recovery of tiger populations in protected reserves in earlier decades had not been documented accurately, and, these population recoveries had not been tracked and linked to the management measures that generated them with any degree of scientific credibility. As a result, to most conservationists, protective measures that had recovered tiger populations in the past, merely seemed like unnecessary, harsh impositions on local people.

There was a clear consensus among the tiger experts who met in London that the knowledge gap in tiger conservation had to be addressed, and scientific knowledge had to be integrated fully with any new conservation initiatives. Tiger conservation has to be based on solid science as well as on a realistic understanding of the social context. Therefore, the success of tiger conservation in the twenty-first century will depend on pursuing a sensible course of action, unaffected either by irrational pessimism or unfounded optimism.

Many new initiatives emerged in the 1990s to promote tiger conservation. A few came from governments in tiger range countries and outside; others were pushed by large international aid agencies. Many initiatives came from international conservation organizations in the non-profit sector. Corporations have backed some efforts. Several non-governmental organizations in tiger range countries have played a catalytic role in these initiatives, as did several dedicated individuals.

These new tiger conservation interventions have assumed several forms: provision of vehicles, boats, communication equipment, firearms, field gear; training reserve staff for active field protection; surveys and scientific research; surveillance of trade; legal measures; conservation education and interfacing with local communities. Some interventions appear to have worked, while others have made no difference. Some well-meant interventions may even have done more harm than good to tigers. It is almost impossible to assess all of these initiatives fairly in a book of this nature. The next chapter looks briefly at some conservation approaches that seem to hold promise for saving wild tigers in the twenty-first century and beyond.

Although captive tigers are useful for public education, their role in saving wild tigers is somewhat limited.

Can We Save The Tiger?

Tigers of the World

Here is an attempt at synthesizing what we know about the ecology of wild tigers with the lessons that we have learnt (or should have learnt) from past conservation efforts. This synthesis tries to show that we cannot predict the tiger's future, using any model that we can construct now. Only purposeful, timely and rational action can ensure that more wild tigers will survive in more places on earth in the future. The key to such action lies in inspiring and rallying public support to the tiger's cause. Virtually anyone in the world can play an important role in this process. Therefore, conservationists should not slide into despondency and inaction in response to the prevalent doomsday prophesies about tigers.

Surprising as it may seem, there are more tigers roaming inside cages in the world today than in their native forests: perhaps as many as three to four times more! Contrary to public perception, it is not difficult to breed captive tigers. Well-managed captive populations have a role in tiger conservation, particularly in educating the public about wild tigers. However, in the overall scheme of helping wild tigers survive, the role of captive tigers is minimal. Releasing captive tigers into their former habitats is not a serious conservation option.

Wild tigers have been extirpated from most places because of habitat loss, over-hunting of prey and poaching of tigers. If these problems are tackled, wild tiger populations can bounce back, as they have repeatedly shown in the past. However, if the problems that eliminated wild tigers in the first place are not adequately addressed, even captive tigers released into such habitats will get wiped out. Simply put, it is cheaper and more effective to recover wild populations of tigers, than to invest a disproportionate amount of the scarce resources in raising captive tigers that have no place to roam in the wild.

Although tiger conservation efforts have been underway for over 50 years, our knowledge of where wild tigers occur is still sketchy. However, given the poorly conceived field surveys used in most areas, this is not surprising. In 1996, the Wildlife Conservation Society and World Wildlife Fund-USA tried to compile available information about where wild tigers occur. They combined satellite maps of forest vegetation with information gathered from knowledgeable individuals in tiger range countries. Although at a rather coarse scale, the resulting maps updated tiger distribution worldwide for the first time. However, even these maps appear to be relatively accurate only for South Asia, where forest fragments are small and a lot more information is available. Ironically, because of data scarcity, the maps actually showed the vast areas of forest cover in Southeast Asia rather than the true extent of tiger distribution. It is clear that a lot more detailed field surveys are needed even to know where wild tigers occur in the world.

The WCS-WWF tiger mapping effort began a process of setting priorities for tiger conservation by demonstrating to the funding agencies that tigers had to be saved in the wild places of Asia, and not in captive enclosures in the west. Secondly, rather than focusing on saving the putative 'subspecies' of tigers, the WCS-WWF approach urged conserving a representative diversity of local adaptations of tigers across their range. The WCS-WWF report categorized priority areas, based on habitat size, fragmentation and threats to tigers, but emphasized that even small tiger populations could potentially be recovered. The bioregions and habitat blocks termed 'Tiger Conservation Units'

Well-designed zoo exhibits can give visitors a good idea of the tiger's natural habitats.

(TCU) identified in the above report are recognized as useful cornerstones in setting up priorities for global tiger conservation.

Tigers now occur in six distinct bioregions that overlap 13 countries. The Indian subcontinent bioregion (including India, Nepal, Bhutan and Bangladesh) encompasses five broad categories of tiger habitats: alluvial grasslands, mangroves, subtropical and temperate upland forests, tropical moist deciduous forests, tropical dry deciduous forests and tropical moist evergreen forests. The Indochina bioregion (Myanmar, Thailand, Laos, Cambodia and Vietnam) has almost similar tiger habitat types. The tiger habitats in Southeast Asia bioregion (peninsular Malaysia and the Indonesian island of Sumatra) are tropical moist evergreen forests and the habitats in the South China bioregion are in subtropical and temperate upland forests. Tiger habitats in the Russian Far East comprise of boreal taiga and temperate mixed conifer-broadleaf forests.

The estimated total area under TCUs in the five bioregions adds up to an impressive figure about 528,300 sq miles (1,368,300 sq km): 160,230 sq miles (415, 000 sq km) in the Indian subcontinent, 242,080 sq miles (627,000 sq km) in Indochina, 63,500 sq miles (164,508 sq km) in Southeast Asia, 60,230 sq miles (156,000 sq km) in the Russian Far East and 2300 sq miles (6000 sq km) in Southern China. Although tigers are in trouble almost everywhere, there are extensive areas in the world where they can still hold out and recover. If tigers are truly protected even in a small proportion of this potential habitat, their populations can bounce back and be secure once again.

Sustaining Tiger Landscapes

A crude analysis shows that current nature reserves form barely 20 per cent of the total tiger habitat in the 13 tiger range countries and less than five per cent of their land area. Tiger conservation in the future has to be built around improving the protection for this relatively small fraction of the land.

The most important task of conservationists will be to convince the public and the decision-makers that dismantling protection measures over such a small fraction of the area in response to local pressures would doom the tiger to extinction. The public has to understand that what is at stake here is not just the loss of a valuable cultural icon like the tiger, but also the permanent forfeiture of many practical economic and social benefits that these protected nature reserves can provide, as we saw in Chapter I. There are no other, easier, shortcuts to tiger conservation.

Only a serious social and political commitment to protected areas can ensure the enforcement of anti-hunting laws, reduction of forest and biomass exploitation and habitat fragmentation. Such protective measures will necessarily include setting up armed patrols and intelligence-gathering systems to prevent illegal incursions, and elimination of developmental projects, livestock grazing, logging and other forest product collection. They will also have to involve voluntary, incentive-driven schemes for resettling people away from core tiger breeding areas, and, where feasible, land purchases and acquisitions to consolidate habitats and enhance landscape connectivity.

All the above actions involve major decisions that have a strong bearing not just on the tigers, but also on people living near and far away from them. Over the tiger's vast range, the authority to make these decisions may vest with military or civilian governments, elected or traditional local authorities, and, rarely, with individuals or collectives of private landowners. Often political power may be split between several levels of authority. The authorities making decisions may have been democratically chosen, inherited power through social tradition or simply seized it by force. There will always be differences in

perception among conservationists as to which form of authority should manage the protected areas.

The above differences in social perceptions, however, in no way detract from the central argument that tigers ecologically need strictly protected preserves in at least a small fraction of their already restricted range. Without a genuine commitment of the authorities in power to truly protected reserves, tigers simply cannot survive in the long run. Their extirpation over most of their range as a result of incompatible human activities proves this point beyond a shadow of doubt.

As we have seen, tigers are landscape animals; they range beyond protected areas to form meta-populations linked by corridors in various stages of disintegration. The pressures on tiger landscapes arise not just because people are greedy, but also because their livelihood needs often clash with the tiger's ecological needs. If the pressures that people are currently imposing on tiger habitats are to be reduced in the future, landscapes outside these habitats have to be made sufficiently productive to meet the resource needs of humans. Therefore, preservation of protected areas can be viable in the long run only if appropriate social, economic and developmental policies lead to land-management practices that reduce human impacts on reserves.

Sometimes, larger economic forces, unrelated to conservation goals, may induce such positive land-use changes and relieve pressures. More often, economic forces exacerbate pressures on tiger reserves. Potentially, the agents who usher in land-use changes can be many: governments, corporations, individual farmers, local entrepreneurs or even international aid agencies.

Integrated conservation and development projects have often been proclaimed as potential harbingers of positive land-use changes. However, current experience with such projects around Indian tiger habitats suggests that these heavily funded efforts have failed to induce land-use changes beneficial to tigers. In some cases, they have even exacerbated pressures. The social mechanisms by which we can create landscapes beneficial to tigers are currently the topics of much debate and discord among conservationists.

Generating Public Support for Tigers

Tigers cannot change their basic biological traits, such as large body size, carnivorous diet and secretive behavior; but these are the very traits that cause human-tiger conflicts. Securing the future of wild tigers will necessarily have to involve major changes in how we humans behave towards tigers. It is difficult to change human attitudes, particularly when survival needs of tigers come into head-on conflict with the livelihood requirements of people living next to them.

The desired change in human attitudes towards tigers is necessary at several different levels. First and foremost attitudes must change among local people such as rural laborers, farmers and traders who live in and around tiger habitats, whose interests often directly clash with those of tigers. These communities often derive substantial and immediate economic benefits by exploiting (albeit unsustainably) tiger habitats. Therefore, attitude change is often most difficult to achieve at this local scale.

A change in attitude is required in other sections of society, too: managers controlling tiger habitats who have to forego lucrative exploitative practices, and instead focus on unpleasant tasks like law enforcement and protection; other government officials whose job it often is to implement developmental projects in tiger habitats; men in business and industry — including the 'smokeless' ecotourism industry — whose enterprises and profit motives may be at odds with what the tiger needs in its last refuges. Finally, there are those millions of consumers of products that come from the tiger's habitats, who are linked to tigers through local, regional and global markets. Consumers of products as diverse as game and domestic animal meat, dairy products, firewood, timber and a host of non-timber forest products as varied as pickles, cigars and shampoos; consumers who may not even be aware how they are adversely affecting tigers.

Tiger ecologist John Seidensticker identified the key to changing human attitudes as 'making a living tiger worth more than a dead one to people'. However, as we saw above, people who have impacts on tigers are many, and their needs are varied. So an array of different tactics have to be used to try to change their perceptions of the relative worth of living and dead tigers. The key is to remember that not everyone can perceive the worth of tigers purely in economic terms. If conservationists try to define and explain the worth of tigers in purely economic terms regardless of the context, they are likely to fail. Depending on whom they are addressing, they would be wise to define the worth of tigers in different ways.

In a few situations it may be possible to demonstrate that local people can derive direct economic benefits from tigers, and enthuse them to support conservation. More often than not, this is difficult in practice. Unlike the wildlife of the African savannas, which lives on relatively poor land incapable of generating large incomes other than through tourism, tiger habitats in Asia are productive forests, which can generate greater cash incomes from being logged or farmed. Also, the human populations around tiger reserves are at much higher densities and comprise of highly stratified, complex societies. Identifying the individual beneficiaries among them, and equitably sharing benefits derived from tiger conservation, is often practically impossible.

Therefore, it may often be fruitful to define the worth of tigers in terms of non-monetary, but tangible long-term practical benefits that the local society will derive from tiger conservation – such as soil and water protection, potential value of genetic resources, and esthetic values – to generate public support.

The tiger has been a very powerful cultural and religious symbol over much of Asia. It still arouses awe and respect among Asian people, particularly in southern Asia. It is very important to use the tiger's cultural appeal – its intrinsic value – as a measure of its worth, when appealing for public support. Although both hunt and kill animals, the attitude of the Asian farmer towards a tiger is very different from that of a New World rancher towards jaguars. Asian cultural attitudes, if harnessed skillfully, can be a powerful means of rallying public support for tigers.

Measuring Success and Failure

It is by now clear that conservation of wild tigers is a complex business: it involves many players, as well as innocent and not-so-innocent bystanders. The strategies and tactics we need to employ are many. Although the tiger remains the ecologically fragile carnivore it has always been, the landscapes, the economies, and the human societies that surround the animal are undergoing dramatic and rapid changes. In the coming decades, tiger conservation is going to be an even more complex business than it has been in the last 50 years.

To be truly successful, like all other businesses, the tiger conservation business must constantly evaluate and measure where it is headed. Just as any normal business measures its profits in dollars, and failures in dollars lost, tiger conservationists must also draw up their balance sheets using a valid currency. All too often conservationists, too, have tried to use dollars (or pounds, rupees or roubles), to measure success. They often proclaim success based on how much money they have raised or spent in saving tigers. At other times, the level of temporary enthusiasm generated – say the number of school

children in a rally for the tiger – is used as a measure of success. Some conservation and development agencies even try to measure success in terms of rural incomes generated, resources extracted, wealth and employment created.

However, the global experience of 50 years of tiger conservation suggests that all these surrogate measures are at best unsatisfactory yardsticks. They may tell us we are succeeding, leading us astray, even when our efforts are failing and tigers continue to decline in the wild.

We need more direct measures of success or failure in tiger conservation. Our central goal is not to raise or spend money, nor to create wealth, employment and human happiness. These are merely tools or by-products in pursuit of the goal to recover populations of wild tigers from the brink of extinction. Therefore, conservation strategies must have a strong built-in component of the reliable monitoring of tigers themselves.

Ecological monitoring of tigers must necessarily take place at several spatial scales. At the landscape level, we need to monitor how tiger habitats are shrinking or expanding and maintaining connectivity; at the level of critical individual tiger populations or reserves we need to know whether populations are increasing, decreasing, or stable. We need to know how vital life-history parameters like survival, recruitment and dispersal between populations are faring. We also need to continuously monitor the impacts of human activities on tigers, their prey base and habitats. These are complex tasks that can only be addressed by applying reliable scientific tools. As we have already seen, in many cases such methods may not even need large resources or advanced technologies. However, in all cases, they need a serious commitment to good science.

One problem with past monitoring efforts over most of tiger range appears to have been the monopolization of the effort by government bureaucracies. Most of these monitoring efforts have not been very successful in generating either valid data or rigorous population assessments. As of now, almost all the reliable scientific data and successes in tiger monitoring have been generated from a handful of research projects in Nepal, India and Russia, which have been carried out by scientists, either on their own or in partnership with governments. Increasing the involvement of non-governmental volunteer naturalists, working in collaboration with scientists, seems to be another powerful approach to monitoring tigers in the future.

Can We Save the Tiger?

A theme that I have revisited several times in this book is the fascination that tigers have aroused in human cultures throughout history. Even now, people everywhere are interested in the fate of tigers. I meet such people all the time, all over the world. A deep sense of hopelessness – that it may be too late to save the tiger – appears to permeate their thoughts. Although they are truly saddened by the tiger's plight, the animal seems like a lost cause to them. As a leading Hong Kong weekly put it, tigers are like old buildings, slated for demolition anyway. When I disagree with such despondency, I have even been accused of being a hopeless optimist. Is the tiger truly a lost cause?

Scientists have long recognized that models of complex systems that can actually predict the future are very difficult to build, even when a large amount of information about the current state of the system is available. This is because sheer chance plays a huge role in what happens in the future. Such predictive models become virtually impossible to build when human will and action are their major components. What happens in the future depends hugely not just on what is

A serious commitment to truly protected areas is essential to secure the tiger's future.

happening now, but also on how we react to the present.

Tiger conservation can be compared to an extremely complex system, with many variables affected by chance and human will. No one can predict with certainty what its state will be a century from now. But what we know is this: our actions and inactions now will have a great impact on where and how many tigers will ultimately survive.

Seventy years ago, hunter naturalist Jim Corbett predicted that India's wild tigers would go extinct within a few decades. Assuming, for argument's sake, that scientists had possessed the necessary data and built predictive models of different tiger populations in Asia in the early 1960s, their predictions would have indicated certain extinction for all of them. Consider the factors that worked against tigers: guerrilla wars and civil strife swept Indochina, China and Indonesia; famines ravaged south Asia, killing people by the thousands. Tigers were retreating under immense pressure from habitat destruction and over-hunting, everywhere.

Indeed, tiger populations in Java and the Caspian region did go extinct as could be predicted. On the other hand, many other populations, even in the countries worst affected by strife and famine, did not blink out; they formed the nuclei for the subsequent tiger population recovery that occurred in the 1970s.

Small populations, perhaps with only four or five breeding tigresses – doomed to extinction by any decent predictive model – recovered and expanded in places like Chitwan, Kanha, Ranthambore and Nagarahole. If the managers of these areas had not acted rationally, these tiger populations would have gone extinct. After 1993, a tiger population in Ranthambore, almost given up for lost by most of its staunchest supporters following the killing of over 18 animals by poachers, recovered dramatically thanks to the efforts of a dedicated wildlife manager and his staff who put their lives on the line for tigers.

In all the above cases, the biological resilience of tigers is certainly a major reason for the population recovery. But human interventions certainly played a greater role. Whether it is a proximate response, such as effective patrolling, or a more distant one like the development of new agricultural techniques that slow down the rate of habitat encroachment, human actions have mattered decisively, but in quite unpredictable ways, in saving the tiger during the last century.

The hard work of conservationists, governments, and enlightened political leaderships, did manage to arrest the tiger's slide in some places at least. In my opinion it was this sense of purpose, focus and optimism that conservationists brought to their campaigns in the 1970s to save the tiger, that really mattered in the end. If wild tigers do not survive the twenty-first century, it will be largely because we, the current crop of tiger conservationists, have lost this sense of purpose, clarity of thinking and sense of hope. By failing to inspire the next generation of tiger conservationists, the present-day doomsayers may be making self-fulfilling prophesies.

What Can We Do?

We have already seen what needs to be done to save wild tigers: establishing protected reserves and buffering them with compatible land uses; de-linking tiger habitats from the forces of market-driven commerce; enlisting sufficient public support for tigers both locally and globally to ensure these goals are met.

These are huge tasks, ones to which almost anyone in the world can contribute meaningfully. And they indeed have, as examples given in this book show. Of course, people living next to tigers, wildlife managers, decision makers, scientists and conservationists working in tiger range countries can contribute most directly to the tiger's cause. Others living far away can support tigers indirectly – by backing conservation

*The elimination of poaching, logging and cattle grazing led to
recoveries of tiger populations within a decade in many reserves of India and Nepal.*

The powerful image of the tiger imprinted in the human mind must now be harnessed effectively to save tigers.

efforts with money, volunteering time, resources and moral support. Almost anyone who pays taxes, receives dividends, contributes to charity, informs others – and above all consumes products that come from tigers' natural habitats – can play a role in saving the big cat.

However, saving the tiger is not just a matter of caring deeply; to be really useful to wild tigers, our interventions in their support have to be careful, well-informed ones. Ironically, because we are now being flooded by a surfeit of news and entertainment in the media, it has become more difficult to decide which interventions to 'save tigers' are wise and which ones are not. I can give a few examples to illustrate this point.

Hundreds of thousands of dollars are being spent by many people keeping tigers in captivity. With the exception of a few good zoos with effective conservation programs, the belief that this activity somehow contributes to tiger conservation is entirely mistaken. The same money, had it been spent in addressing the pressing problems faced by wild tigers, would have been of real help to the species. Every time a tiger dies in a badly run zoo or menagerie, the Internet is flooded with news stories, exposés and outrage from people who care deeply about tigers. However, all this outpouring of care and anger means nothing for the future survival of tigers in the wild.

Millions of dollars are being spent on developmental projects around tiger habitats by large aid agencies and private charities, in the name of human progress and economic development. Some of these projects are in fact doing immense harm to the survival prospects of tigers and their habitat. Citizens of wealthy nations who pay the taxes or donations that eventually support many of these projects are usually unaware of their involuntary contribution to the decline of the tiger.

Millions of dollars' worth of forest products ranging all the way from wild honey, spices, shampoos, incense sticks, and hardwood timber, are consumed by ever-increasing numbers of urban consumers far away from the tiger forests. How many of these consumers know that, more often than not, the use of these harmless-looking products contributes to the eventual extirpation of tigers, as surely as the consumption of their body parts in a Chinese apothecary's store would?

Big corporations are extracting billions of dollars' worth of resources and profits out of the Asian wilderness, which is the tiger's only home. Many of them – selling anything from breakfast cereals to varnish paint – use the tiger as a powerful marketing icon. Yet, with a few honorable exceptions, most such businesses do not contribute much to the tigers' cause. Their executives would not be as unconcerned if the shareholders who ultimately own these companies, forced them to look beyond the financial bottom line and actively help the cause of wild tigers.

The above are just a few examples of actions or simple inactions that can help or harm the cause of wild tigers. We can find many more examples, if we look around carefully. Therefore, the first thing anyone who cares deeply about saving wild tigers effectively should do is to become well informed before intervening. I know this from the following experience:

Teamwork Saves Tigers

When I began to study tigers in Nagarahole reserve in Karnataka State, India, in the 1980s, with support from the Wildlife Conservation Society, I had already been familiar with the park's problems for over a decade. I had worked closely with K. M. Chinnappa, a ranger in the forestry department, who had played a dominant role in resurrecting Nagarahole during the 1970s by confronting local poachers, timber thieves, squatters and illegal graziers. Even as prey and tiger populations recovered under his strict protection, deep antagonism had built up between the park staff and local people who were often instigated by criminal elements. In 1992, this antagonism culminated in a major riot in which the park staff were assaulted and forests were burnt by an invading mob, leading to Chinnappa's resignation from his job.

However, as I conducted my research and he administered his range, we had jointly built a network of keen young men from neighboring districts who volunteered to help with the fieldwork. After the riot in 1992, this network swung into action and ensured that the culprits were brought to book. In 1993, with support from the Wildlife Conservation Society and Global Tiger Patrol, we initiated a conservation education project specifically targeting students and young people who lived around Nagarahole. Soon the influence of our network expanded, and public support for the criminals who poached and smuggled timber collapsed. This made the enforcement of park rules and wildlife protection easier for the park staff.

A major problem facing the long-term survival of Nagarahole as critical tiger habitat is the presence inside the park of several hundred families of disenfranchised and poor tribal people. For decades they had been demanding from the government provision of housing, power supply, land for farming and other amenities inside the park. The problem was that provision of such facilities would fragment the park and further aggravate the conflict between wildlife and people; of course, it was also illegal. To address this problem, in the mid 1990s our conservation network, now formally named 'Wildlife First', began interacting with local social activists and political leaders to find a pragmatic solution to this pressing problem. Working in close cooperation with the State and Federal Governments, Wildlife First played a catalytic role in advancing a voluntary resettlement project, in which over 200 families moved out of the park into resettlement areas where their demands for land and social amenities were met. This project is currently progressing.

To address the problems of deteriorating park protection in view of the government's budget constraints, in the face of increased threats to tigers, the Wildlife Conservation Society, with support from Save the Tiger Fund, jointly promoted by Exxon Corporation and the National Fish and Wildlife Foundation (NFWF), helped us to initiate the Karnataka Tiger Conservation Project in four prime tiger habitats in Karnataka. The project provided 20 patrol vehicles, three patrol boats, wireless equipment, field gear, insurance cover, incentives and training to over 1000 forest department staff.

The Karnataka Tiger Conservation Project also intensified conservation education work among local communities around these four parks, trying to nurture future community leaders who would care for the tiger, with no other motive than a belief in the animal's inherent value, and its right to survive on this planet.

Through my long-term scientific research on tigers and prey in these parks, I continue to monitor this unique example of local pride and commitment to tigers, supported by conservationists from across the world. I believe that the potential for such ecologically rational and socially responsible collaborations is great. Therefore, I believe that wild tigers are not yet a lost cause. But all of us must act sensibly to save tigers before it is too late.

If this book contributes in some small measure to honestly informing readers about critical issues in tiger conservation, without making them lose hope in the future of the magnificent predator, I will be more than satisfied.

There is reason to believe that wild tigers are not yet a lost cause.

TIGER HABITAT

CURRENT/POTENTIAL HABITAT

RANGE - 1900

Source for tiger range information: Wildlife Conservation Society/World Wildlife Fund-USA

Classification

Class:	*Mammalia*
Order:	*Carnivora*
Family:	*Felidae*
Genus:	*Panthera*
Scientific Name:	*Panthera tigris* (Linnaeus, 1758)

Traditionally classified into eight subspecies, but only the following two or three may be valid: *Tigris* (in mainland Asia), *Sumatrae* (in Sumatra), and *Virgata* (extinct form from West Asia).

Body Size and Structure

Total length: males	106-122 in (270-310 cm)
females	95-105 in (240-265 cm)
Shoulder height:	36-44 in (90-110 cm)
Weight: males	385-570 lb (175-260 kg)
females	220-385 lb (100-175 kg)
	Tigers from Sumatra are much smaller.

Life History Traits and Ecology

Gestation period:	103-110 days
Litter size:	1 to 7, three cubs being common; sex ratio equal at birth
Age at dispersal:	18-24 months
Maximum life span in the wild:	12-15 years; 20 years or longer in captivity
Prey requirements:	About 40-50 ungulate prey animals per year for maintenance and about 60-70 such prey per year for a tigress raising cubs

Some International Agencies Supporting Tiger Conservation

Wildlife Conservation Society (WCS), New York, U.S.A. www.wcs.org

World Wide Fund for Nature / World Wildlife Fund (WWF) family of organizations. www.wwf.org

Save The Tiger Fund of the National Fish and Wildlife Foundation and ExxonMobil Corporation, Washington DC, U.S.A. www.nfwf.org

US Fish and Wildlife Service – Rhinoceros and Tiger Conservation Fund, Washington DC, U.S.A. http:\\international.fws.gov

21st Century Tiger: A consortium of Global Tiger Patrol, Zoological Society of London and Esso Petroleum, London, UK. www.zsl.org

INDEX

*Entries in **bold** indicate pictures*

Recommended Reading

Literature that deals with tigers is vast and varied, as befits an animal that holds human culture in its thrall. Such writings range all the way from ancient legends to hunters' tales; from impassioned advocacy to technical monographs; glorious pictorial books to equation-studded scientific papers. My list tries to capture some of the diversity of writings on tigers and is undoubtedly biased towards the factual over the fanciful:

Man-eaters of Kumaon by Jim Corbett. Oxford University Press, London, 1944. Adventures of hunting man-eating tigers in the Himalayan foothills during the first half of the twentieth century.

The Deer and the Tiger by George Schaller. University of Chicago Press, Chicago, 1967. A report of the first-ever scientific study of wild tigers, written in brilliant prose that makes the jungles of central India come alive.

Tiger Moon by Fiona and Melvin Sunquist. University of Chicago Press, Chicago, 1988. A popular book that captures the essence of a decade-long scientific study in Chitwan Park, Nepal.

Tigers: The Secret Life by Valmik Thapar. Rodale Press, Emmaus, 1989. Observations on wild tigers in Ranthambore, with stunning photographs by Fateh Singh Rathore.

How the Tiger Lost its Stripes by Cory Meacham. Harcourt Brace & Company, New York 1997. An engaging account of current tiger conservation issues, with a slant on the politics among tiger conservationists.

Through the Tiger's Eyes by Stan Breedan and Belinda Wright. Ten Speed Press, Berkeley, 1996. Beautifully illustrated book on tiger conservation with an emphasis on the issue of illegal trade and its control.

The Year of the Tiger by Michael Nichols and Geoffrey Ward. National Geographic Press, Washington DC, 1998. A pictorial overview of tiger conservation prospects, interwoven with observations on the life of a wild tigress in central India.

Riding the Tiger: Tiger Conservation in Human-dominated Landscapes. Edited by John Seidensticker, Sarah Christie and Peter Jackson. Cambridge University Press, Cambridge, 1999. An authoritative, illustrated compilation of articles providing 'state of the art' knowledge about tiger biology and conservation issues.

Tigers by John Seidensticker, Worldlife Library, Colin Baxter Photography, 1996.

Acknowledgments

A book like this must necessarily draw on the work of many scientists and conservationists. While I thank them all collectively, my indebtedness to the following individuals must be acknowledged: George Schaller, John Eisenberg and John Seidensticker, who shaped my thinking about carnivores; K. M. Chinnappa, Melvin Sunquist, Fiona Sunquist and Jim Nichols, who helped me acquire the varied skills necessary to study and understand tigers. I also thank Geoffrey Ward, Samba Kumar, Praveen Bhargav, George Nicholson and the publishers for their assistance in making this book a reality.